JOG ON
JOURNAL

BELLA MACKIE

JOG ON JOURNAL

A Practical Guide to Getting Up and Running

WILLIAM
COLLINS

William Collins
An imprint of HarperCollins*Publishers*
1 London Bridge Street
London SE1 9GF

www.WilliamCollinsBooks.com

First published in Great Britain in 2019 by William Collins

1

Illustrations by Anna Morrison

A catalogue record for this book is available from the British Library

ISBN 978-0-00-837003-9

Printed and bound by CPI Group (UK) Ltd, Croydon, CR0 4YY

This book is produced from independently certified FSC™ paper
to ensure responsible forest management

Find out more about HarperCollins and the environment at
www.harpercollins.co.uk/green

For everyone
who got in contact with me
after *Jog On* came out and trusted me
with their mental health stories –
this journal is for you

INTRODUCTION

Hello. Welcome to my diary – where I'll be writing down my innermost secrets and talking about boys I fancy.

Oh no, wait, this isn't that kind of journal. This is a journal for YOU. And while you're welcome to write about boys (or girls) as much as you want in it, I'll be focusing more on mental health and how running might be able to help you. Some of you 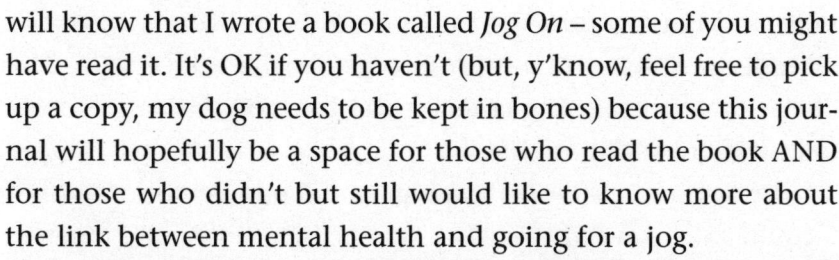 will know that I wrote a book called *Jog On* – some of you might have read it. It's OK if you haven't (but, y'know, feel free to pick up a copy, my dog needs to be kept in bones) because this journal will hopefully be a space for those who read the book AND for those who didn't but still would like to know more about the link between mental health and going for a jog.

Jog On is a book I wrote about my experience with anxiety – a horrible condition which makes life feel incredibly scary and can leave you feeling unable to cope with the everyday.

I wrote it to show other sufferers that they are not alone, and to promote jogging as one tool to help with such issues. For me, running made me feel stronger than I ever had, it gave me back some independence (which mental illness often robs from you) and it showed me how strong the link between my brain and my body is – a link I think we often ignore in the modern world.

In five years of running, I've stopped having the panic attacks which paralysed me. I've been able to go to places that my anxious brain would've prevented me from visiting. I've taken on challenges that I would've hidden away, and I've graduated from a life half lived to one that feels full and exciting – not tinged with fear and endless panic. I still have moments of anxiety and low mood – after all, running is not a cure-all (nothing is) – but I'm mostly able to dig myself out of these moments now, and for that, I credit my daily jogs. I can draw a direct line from that first short run I took to where I am now, and I'm far from the only person to feel this way. As the legendary runner and author George Sheehan once said: 'The obsession with running is really an obsession with the potential for more and more life.'[1]

The response to *Jog On* was bigger and more emotional than I could ever have dreamed. I wrote it honestly and openly, hoping that it might help a few people and make my family understand my brain a bit better. But it ended up being a best-seller, and I've had thousands of messages from people who read it, either telling me about their own battles with mental health or asking for tips about how to get into running. It made me realise that one person being really honest about their mental health can produce a knock-on effect. Being blunt about my weirdest thoughts and scariest moments seemed to help other people open up and talk about theirs. It's a hard thing to do – especially when you feel as though other people will judge you or recoil. But it's really the only way to shrug off the long-held stigma surrounding mental illness and – more importantly – it's the only way to help yourself. It's nice being alive at a time in history when we're dismantling the traditional stereotypes about mental health, but it's even nicer being able to feel like you can tell an employer, a loved one or a doctor about what you're going through without fear of mockery or anger.

Despite knowing how important it is to open up to others when we're feeling low or worried, sometimes it's still hard to actually do it. I told parts of my story to different people for years – shading in bits and holding back certain details depending on what I felt the other person could handle. And sometimes you just want to have a place to talk about this stuff without having to manage another person's expectations. So this journal will be an honest place to do that. A space to learn a bit more about mental health, somewhere to start or further your running journey, a place to reassess what you want from running and, most importantly, a home for all the thoughts you want to get out.

There's a good reason that people have kept diaries for centuries. Though he was far from the first, Samuel Pepys is

probably the most well-known diarist.[2]
He jotted his thoughts down for ten years
between 1660 and 1669 and wrote over a
million words – many about his mistresses.
(Maybe it assuaged a guilty conscience.
If it did, he hid it well.) Cognitive
behavioural therapy also encourages
the subject to write down their thoughts
– a form of brain homework if you like.
More on that later.

Pepys might not have made the link between his obsessive record keeping and his own mental health but modern
research has. Brain scans have shown a change in the amygdala
– the part of the brain responsible for processing our emotions
– when we put pen to paper about our worries.[3] Studies have
even shown us that writing down our negative thoughts and
emotions might help our physical health – prompting fewer
trips to the GP and leading to less time off work.[4]

Think of it like a Pensieve (if you've not read *Harry Potter*
then firstly, wow, and also, a Pensieve is a stone dish you can
put your memories in when you feel like your mind is over-
flowing with them) – somewhere to offload the stuff that's
worrying you and look at it from a place slightly removed.[5] A
thought whirring around your mind gets gloopy and collects
detritus as it goes round and round, making it hard to rational-
ise. But by looking at the thought summed up on paper, we're
able to see it more clearly and – hopefully – let go of the anxiety
around it.

I received so many questions from readers when *Jog On* came out, questions about running, about panic attacks, about how to motivate yourself when it feels impossible, about the best running trainers and even about what ice cream I eat after a jog. So many of these queries will be addressed in the coming chapters – because there's nothing better than a gaggle of avid readers to tell you what's important and what you've missed. It's been like free market research and I'm so glad of it. Lastly, I am not in the business of motivational quotes or cheery platitudes. I still struggle from time to time – I don't live amongst glitter and rainbows.

So this might be a touch more cynical than some journals – but if that's your thing, then welcome to your running and mental health journal.

One last note – since I've tried to tie together advice on running *and* discussion of mental health, I've decided that this journal will alternate between the two. Obviously the sections will merge in lots of places, but I think it's helpful to concentrate solely on mental health in some places – after all, what's more important? And equally, when we're talking about running shoes or how to prevent injury, I'd like you to be focusing on that without getting bogged down in symptoms about anxiety. But you can't understand why running helps boost mood unless we also look at the times when your mental health is suffering. Also, feel free to read just the running parts or just the mental stuff if that's what you want to do. My mum read only the peace bits of *War and Peace*. She is excellent.

SECTION ONE

MENTAL HEALTH

PART ONE

GETTING HELP

This journal talks a lot about mental health – which covers a HUGE range of issues. I'm going to mainly talk about anxiety because that's my wheelhouse (I would smash *Mastermind* if excessive worry was my specialist subject), but that itself is an umbrella term. And mental-health issues often overlap, so

I think that you'll recognise much of this stuff whether you suffer from OCD, social anxiety or panic attacks. All of us afflicted with anxiety speak the same language. And that's true of runners too. And anxious runners are even more in sync with each other. When I do talks, there's usually a book signing at the end, and I usually ask people whether they're anxious, a runner or an anxious runner. Because those are my people. They're not coming to see me because they love poetry and fine dining.

I assume you're here because you're also in one of those three tribes (you can like poetry and food too, of course).

First things first. If you're struggling with your brain and haven't sought help – go and speak to your GP. This book – NO book – can do more for you than talking to a professional who can help you with diagnosis, therapy, medication and support. It's hard. A 2004 study by the World Health Organization (WHO) found that between 30 and 80 per cent of people with a mental-health issue don't seek treatment – and the reasons why vary.[1] If you've not sought any help, circle the explanation(s) that fit this best:

Shame

A feeling that you're not worth help

A sense that nothing can make you feel better

Not knowing where to go

Not feeling confident that your story will be confidential

A worry that you can't access or afford treatment

A feeling that you won't be taken seriously

A bad experience with a GP or other medical professional

You want to handle it alone

If your reason isn't listed, write it in the space below.

What makes you worried
about getting help?

I understand all of these concerns, by the way – I've felt nearly all of them myself. But here's the thing: mental illness will not go away on its own, and the longer it continues, the harder it can be to treat. We know that many mental-health conditions manifest in adolescence, and calcify over time. If you seek help you could:

- Lower your risk of further incidents down the road.
- Reduce career and life disruption.
- Remove the need for longer treatment or hospitalisation.
- Gain the tools to help you cope with future stressful periods.
- Learn how to talk to loved ones about how you're feeling.

If that all seems a bit clinical, what if I told you that getting help might make you feel BETTER, see glimmers of hope and no longer have to shoulder the burden of worry and panic and sadness?

Write down what you'd most like to achieve with some help – for me it was reducing panic attacks and loosening the grip that intrusive 'what if' thoughts had on my brain. Yours might be feeling happier, or reducing obsessions, or being able to go on planes.

Seeking professional help for the first time can feel daunting and as though you're not in control. So it might be helpful to keep one or two things in mind. If you're nervous about going to your GP, consider taking a friend to hold your hand and,

What would you like to get from some help?

most importantly, remember that doctors see people who are struggling mentally EVERY DAY. One in four people are said to experience some mental-health problems in their lifetime, and your doctor is on the frontline of initial treatment. The other thing to say is that if you don't feel satisfied with the help you're offered then ask for a different doctor or enquire about other services on offer. Look, it happens, some doctors aren't fully *au fait* with mental-health problems, just like some employers aren't and some mothers. But their numbers are shrinking and you have every right to sensitive and humane treatment. So if it's not working for you, don't lose heart, just try a different tack.

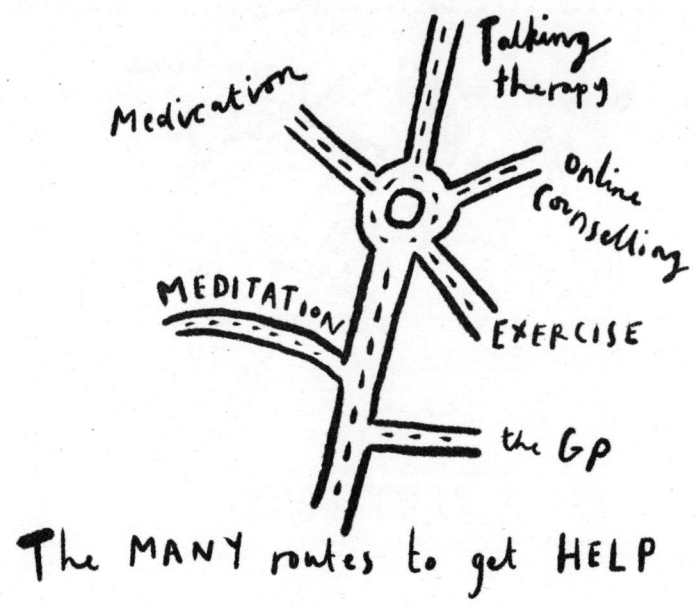

The MANY routes to get HELP

That probably sounded a bit bossy. But it's important to speak to a professional about mental health first of all. There are so many people out there pushing wacky cures for anxiety and depression, and they normally do absolutely nothing to help people. But desperate people are prone to try anything – I once bought a VERY expensive set of vitamins that online testimonials promised would cure my anxiety. They didn't even make my hair shiny.

PART TWO

THE ANXIETY UMBRELLA

Anxiety is a mother-fucker. It's not mild niggles about a work task or a slight panic about the iron having been left on. It's all-encompassing – a worry about a work task multiplies, mushrooms and becomes all you can focus on. A vague unease in crowds can end up in panic attacks that feel like you're going to die. A passing thought about germs can end up in an obsession about cleaning. Your brain is on high alert for danger all the time. This is not the same as fear, which is in response to an obvious threat. Anxiety is about future and imagined dangers – most of them enlarged, unrealistic and twisted beyond recognition. Everyone has felt anxious at some point in their lives, but most people don't become consumed by it. Lucky them.

I'm going to give you some personal examples because sharing is caring and I always feel relieved when I hear about other people's experiences (it makes me feel less alone).

Here are two small examples of my anxious brain – the scale of these episodes differs greatly but both were incredibly distressing:

I am on holiday and I walk across some grass. I feel a sting on the sole of my foot and look down to see a wasp. Immediately, I panic. My brain flies straight to the certain knowledge that I will develop anaphylactic shock from this sting. I can't breathe – it's happening fast. I run to the house, and I can feel my lips swelling up, my lungs constricting. I'm clawing at my throat, desperate to get some air in but I can't and we're miles away from help. I signal to my family – frantically trying to make them understand that I'm no longer able to breathe as they try and calm me down. I lie down on the bed as my mum strokes my hair and I wait for death. But ten minutes later I am forced to concede that what I thought was an allergic reaction was a panic attack brought on by my powerfully anxious brain. I'm so wiped out by it, and so embarrassed and sad that this is where my mind goes, that I have to have a two-hour nap. That fear of anaphylaxis stayed with me for a further two years. I wasn't twelve by the way, I was twenty-nine.

Can you think of a time when your anxiety went from zero to a hundred in seconds? It's good to get it out – I can look back and laugh about it (a bit) now and the more I tell people these stories, the less powerful they seem. No, the less powerful they ARE.

A time when your ANXIETY ramped up in seconds

Right, scenario number two:

I am at college and the bus journey was a bit weird, I felt hot and dizzy and things felt 'off'. When I get to the building, I feel ill and scared and everything looks weird. I panic – but not about anything in particular and that feels even scarier. I make my excuses and leave to go home. That night my head spins as I try to get my brain around why I felt so strange. I tie myself in knots as I explore stranger and more irrational paths trying to make sense of what I'm experiencing. It's overwhelming doom mixed with a feeling that everything is unreal. And I have no blueprint for that. Eventually I settle on the answer: I must be going mad. Mad like you hear about on *Crimewatch*. Mad like killers in movies. And it clicks – I am psychotic. I have no proof of this, but that's where my mind has landed. From that day, I become obsessed with monitoring my 'mad' behaviour. I pick apart every thought that pops into my mind – am I paranoid? Did I just think someone was watching me? Do I hear voices? The exhaustion from trying to push back against these thoughts is overwhelming and, on top of all the thoughts which keep coming, I'm experiencing a million physical side effects of anxiety too – adrenaline courses through my body, I feel sick constantly, I can't sleep, I can't eat. The mental and physical go hand in hand and egg each other on – it's a vicious cycle.

This one was an even lower moment in my life, but the two stories have a couple of strong similarities. Can you spot them? No, I'm kidding, you're not eight and this isn't *Where's Wally*. I'll tell you:

Catastrophic thinking – my mind (and maybe yours since you're here) has the amazing ability to go from zero to a hundred in two seconds flat. And it's never a positive destination. The only places my mind goes are dark and scary. Catastrophic thinking can be described as your brain searching for the worst-case scenario. It might seem like a self-defence mechanism – 'Prepare for the worst, be pleasantly surprised' – but it actually kick-starts an anxiety

loop. You think about the worst scenario and your brain and body produce a reaction like the one you'd have *if that actual scenario was happening.* So I imagine I'm in serious medical danger, or feel like I'm going mad, and I panic. Adrenaline floods me, I'm tearful, I can't breathe and I think the world is ending. When it doesn't, I don't pick myself up and feel exhilarated that I'm all safe. I feel wiped out and scared for the next time I feel worries like this. This can make you feel like there's no point in feeling hopeful about the future or lead to you skipping situations that produce catastrophic thoughts – thereby feeding the loop and reinforcing this thought pattern.

An inability to self-soothe. No, I'm not a baby and yes, this description is slightly grim, but it's also kind of spot on. In both these cases, I couldn't pull myself back from panic. I didn't push back against the thoughts or calm my body down. I was washed away with the fear, and let it take over. That's natural, your mind tells you there's something to worry about and so you listen. It's a primal thing – this fight-or-flight instinct – but with anxiety, you have to learn that your instincts are often wrong. And that's a hard one to realise – that sometimes your brain and body are working against your best interests. But it's a vital thing to learn – because understanding the difference between real dangers and imagined ones will eventually help stop your mind seeing dangers everywhere and help you decide whether a worry is worth engaging with or not.

Can you write down examples of your anxiety and see what the similarities are? It's good to spot the patterns your worries take, even if they seem completely different initially.

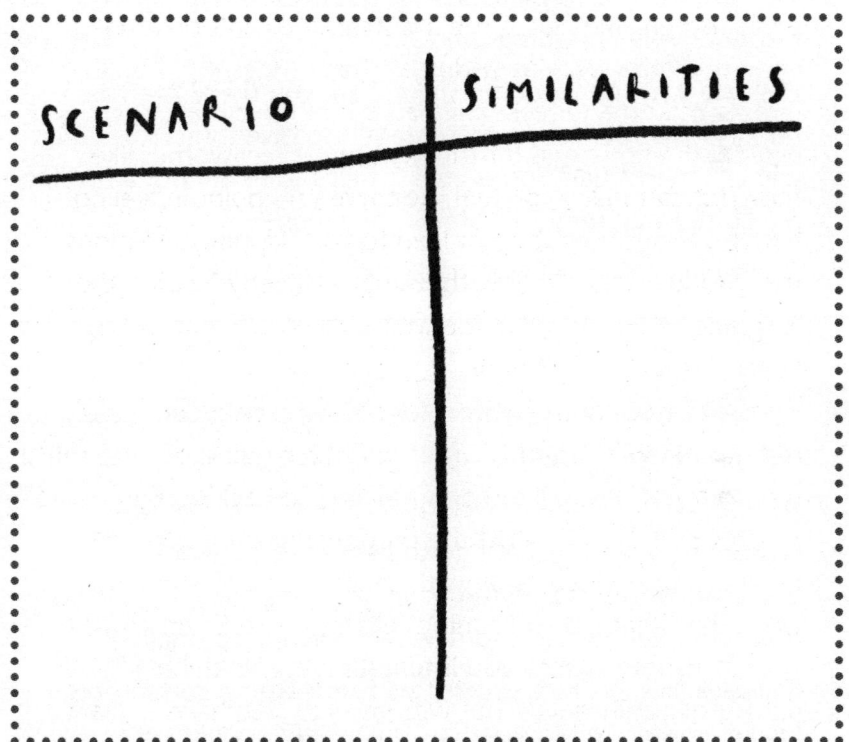

What can you take away from the comparison? Do both scenarios involve a specific place? Or a time when you're tired? Begin to notice what common threads link your worries and remind yourself of them when you next feel anxious.

How can you stop catastrophising? We'll talk about this a lot more as we go on, but here are a few tips:

- Notice what your brain is doing – it's a lot easier to calm yourself down if you catch the pattern early.

- View the thoughts from a distance. It helps me to internally say: 'Ah, I see I am spiralling into doom-laden thoughts. I wonder why I'm going there.'

- Evaluate why you're going there – are you tired? Are you hungry? Do you have a presentation to give tomorrow? Are you pre-menstrual? Sometimes it helps to figure out a real-life fire-lighter that might be stoking the worry.

- Don't berate yourself too much – it never helps to call yourself a dick. Instead, go easy – a sort of 'Thanks for trying, but not today' reply to your mind.

- That said, dispute the worry – don't discount it completely, but question it. I use this with flying: 'But planes are the safest way to travel, Bella.' Might sound small, but it has an impact.

- Figure out what you CAN do to help ease the worry – practical things, like paying a bill or setting aside time to write that presentation. Start somewhere, even if it's small.

- If all else fails, distract yourself with something comforting – I bake or listen to old Agatha Christie audiobooks when my mind is spiralling. Often doing something with your hands can help quieten your mind.

FIGHT   _Flight_

PART THREE

FIGHT-OR-FLIGHT

The term 'fight-or-flight' sounds really dramatic – as though you're about to go to rumble à la _West Side Story_. If you've not seen the film, go and watch it. Tony. That's all I'll say about that.

It's important for people with anxiety (and those with many other mental-health disorders, from PTSD to bipolar) to familiarise themselves with this very normal human reaction, because it comes from fear – and fear is the sensible and reasonable cousin of anxiety. The cousin who calls your grandma on her birthday. The cousin who trained for years and makes your mum wonder why you never became a doctor. And yes, I am stretching this metaphor, thank you for noticing.

Anyway. Fear is healthy – we need it. It's how we know to get out of a burning building. And it does this with the fight-or-flight response. This physical reaction – when the human body produces a bunch of hormones to make you faster and stronger in the event of . . . oh, let's say a lion attack – is a wonderful thing, but our brains respond identically to both real and unreal danger. So the fight-and-flight mode that equips us to fight terrifying animals can also kick in on a Monday morning rush-hour commute when there is no obvious threat. And for people prone to anxiety . . . well, this response can start working against us.

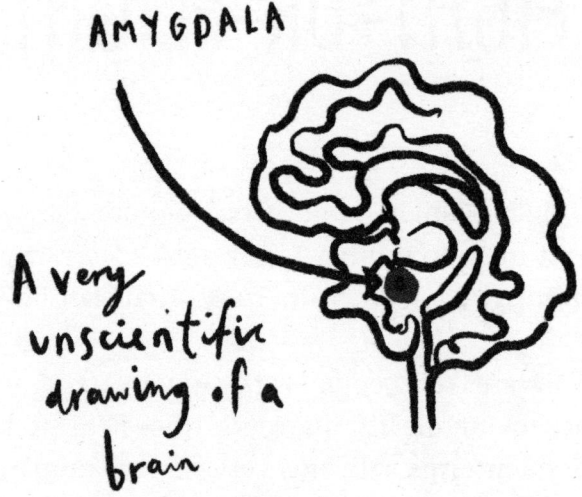

AMYGDALA

A very unscientific drawing of a brain

The fight-or-flight response does a bunch of stuff to your body when it kicks in – your amygdala (the part of the brain which processes emotions) sends out a sort of distress signal and your body knows to gear up for a scary situation. You produce more adrenaline, your heart rate goes up, you breathe faster and you get a rush of energy. It's thought that this all happens before your conscious brain has even considered what's happening (and explains why a person could jump in front of a train to save a person who's fallen on the tracks).[2]

In a scary situation this is all GREAT! But if there's no immediate emergency and yet your brain goes on sending the danger alert, then your body keeps producing the adrenaline and this keeps your brain thinking there's something going wrong. That feeling of excess energy, that pounding heart. Think about how that feels. It's not nice, huh? So of course if you're feeling all of those things, your mind is still casting around for peril. And so the cycle begins.

A thought about something going WRONG

Feel anxious, PANICKED, experience a sense of DREAD

physical signs of ANXIETY

Sound familiar?

It might be helpful here to write down five times your fight-and-flight response has kicked into gear for a GOOD reason. And then write down five times it's reared its head in an unhelpful way. We need to make an effort to distinguish the normal fear reaction from the excessive and unwarranted fear reaction so that our brains are better able to respond appropriately in a future stressful situation.

Just as with catastrophising, you can help push back against this. It's exhausting to get trapped in such a cycle. You spend hours, days, weeks feeling full of adrenaline – teeth grinding, sweating, humming with nerves – and then you crash and can be overwhelmed with headaches, tired to your very bones, feel shaky and achy as though you have the flu. And, long term, cortisol (the stress hormone) isn't very good for you – it's been shown to prompt weight gain, affect blood pressure and mess with cholesterol.[3] And the rest. Anxiety really is the gift which keeps on giving.

5 Times FIGHT or FLIGHT has helped

①

②

③

④

⑤

5 Times FIGHT or FLIGHT has definitely NOT helped

①

②

③

④

⑤

Some things that help put the brakes on this cycle:

- **EXERCISE** (there may . . . just may be more about this later).
- **MEDITATION AND MINDFULNESS.**
- **SOCIALISING** – studies have shown that a 'tend and befriend' response can lower these symptoms of stress – providing safety and security instead of panic.[4]
- **LAUGHTER** – sounds simple, but has been shown to reduce stress hormones and promote mood-elevating hormones like endorphins.[5]

Above all, it helps to reassure yourself. It sounds silly, but sometimes just saying, 'I am safe', as many times as I need to (internally or out loud), can really help calm my body down in moments when I want to get the fuck out of a place that my body is telling me is scary. Try it, see how it feels after you've spoken positively to yourself. Our internal voices are so often complicit in making us feel worse – and it's a 'skill' we build up over many years, so it's understandably hard to break. But with practice, you can make that voice more sympathetic and less willing to just go along with the latest worry that might have popped into your brain. Reassuring yourself is a good way to start. It can be any mantra as long as it's positive and calming – 'I can do this' is another good one.

Write down three things you might say to yourself next time you feel panic rising and keep them at the back of your mind for future use:

THREE THINGS I COULD SAY TO REASSURE MYSELF

①

②

③

PART FOUR

PANIC ATTACKS

Since we've discussed catastrophic thinking and fight-or-flight, let's look at panic attacks – often the end result of the fight-or-flight response. Have you had a panic attack? If you're reading this book, it's likely that you have. Some statistics say that 13 per cent of people have had one in their lifetime.[6] And some people will only have one or two – triggered by a stressful period in their life like a new job or a bereavement. Some people will have tons. At that point, you might have panic disorder. That's an anxiety condition – under the umbrella of issues that anxiety covers. Panic attacks are debilitating. They can make you think you're dying – so often people who experience them initially think there's something seriously wrong physically. When I first experienced them, I thought I was having: a heart attack, a stroke, a brain aneurysm. Often you think you're about to pass out. Let me get this straight first up: YOU ARE NOT GOING TO PASS OUT.

Probably. I'm not a doctor. But many doctors have told me that panic attacks rarely lead to fainting. You might feel dizzy for sure, and the earth might feel like it's moving beneath you, BUT: during a panic attack, your heart beats faster, and your blood pressure rises. When people faint it's normally because of a sudden drop in blood pressure.[7] So strike that off your list of worries. I've had so many panic attacks I could write a thesis on them, and I've never once fainted during an episode. From kissing a boy aged eighteen, sure, but never from a panic attack. Remind yourself of this – it's important! So many people develop a fear that they'll pass out and it can bring on the anxiety cycle we talked about earlier. If you feel wobbly, sit down for sure, drink some water, but don't worry you're going to stack it right outside Starbucks, because you won't.

OK, good – moving on. I'm going to write down a list of panic attack symptoms – and you tick the ones you've experienced.[8] This isn't an exhaustive list but these are the very common ones. It'll be like a fun puzzle exercise, except it's about mental illness and there's no fun involved. Tricked you. OK, GO!

- Dizziness
- A feeling that you can't breathe
- Heart racing
- Sweating or feeling ICE cold
- Blurred vision
- Shaky hands
- A lump in your throat
- A sense of impending DOOM
- A need to flee to safety
- A feeling you're going to faint

- OR DIE
- or go 'crazy'
- Chest pain
- Tingling hands or feet

Truly horrible bloody things. What's your worst symptom? Mine is that I can't breathe. I pull at my throat and gasp a lot. Which makes me think that people must be noticing my freak-out and that can make me more panicky. But here's the thing. Mostly, panic attacks are happening beneath the surface – like when a serene duck is barely moving on the water but actually its feet are frantically paddling. All the things going on in your mind and in your body feel IMMENSE but are normally not visible to a passer-by. Think about how many times you have seen a stranger having an anxiety attack – I've never seen one person experience one and I have them myself. So put that worry out of your head. So many people worry that they'll cause a scene and look stupid when, in actual fact, human beings are really self-absorbed and barely notice anything you're doing unless you fall over. Then they notice, trust me (I fall over a lot).

The irony of it all is that actually a really good thing to do when you're feeling a panic attack coming on is to talk to someone. Make a human connection, look into someone else's eyes and force your brain to concentrate on something else. And this isn't only a practical bit of advice. In my quest to get everyone on earth (I'm grandiose like that) talking about mental health, I think it would be amazingly helpful if we could tell a stranger that we're feeling a bit anxious without feeling silly or 'mad'. If someone told me they were panicking I'd try and be as helpful and reassuring as possible – as would most people, I think. Wouldn't it be lovely if we felt able to do that?

There's lots of advice on how to overcome panic attacks – from your GP to charities like MIND, from eminent psychiatrists to quack practitioners. Some of it's good, some of it's unhelpful. I'm not a professional (at literally anything) so all I can tell you is what works for me. And normally it's a multi-pronged approach – no ONE thing is guaranteed to nail it. What helps is having a toolbox full of things that help and being able to pull them out when needed.

- Focus on your breathing. In situations like this, there's a right way and a wrong way to breathe. You probably take shallow breaths when you start to panic – and many people start to hyperventilate (inhaling deeper or taking quicker breaths than usually).[9] Normally, you breathe in oxygen and breathe out carbon dioxide (hello GCSE science). But when you hyperventilate, the carbon dioxide levels in your bloodstream drop. You start to feel sick or dizzy, and this provokes more panic. So you need to calm your breathing down. Easier said than done, I know. I begin by taking one big breath and telling myself, 'I CAN breathe.' Breathe in through your nose, and put one hand on your chest and one on your stomach. Notice the breath move through your body – you should feel your stomach move but your chest should remain pretty still. Keep doing this for as long as you need to until you're convinced that you can breathe.

- Find a quiet place to sit down. If you feel like you're going to faint (even though you're not), take a seat, but don't hunch up. Keep your chest broad so that you can keep on taking proper breaths.

- Notice your surroundings. It helps me to focus on the sky, or on an interesting building, or to watch a dog walk past. Anything to centre you back in your surroundings.

- Try not to rush away. The instinct is SO strong to get the fuck out and head for 'safety' but, in doing so, you can set up problems for yourself in the future. If you feel scared in a place and leave before you calm down and realise that there's nothing to really fear, then your brain tends to designate that place as 'unsafe'. Then you start to avoid places and your world can get really small really fast. So stick it out if you can. Just as an example, leaving the scene of a panic attack meant that I later avoided:

  – Planes

  – Lifts

  – Busy spaces

– The centre of London

– Sainsbury's

– Theatres and cinemas

– Motorways

– Coaches (not really,
I just don't like coaches.
Not enough toilets)

- Focus on your senses. Touch something soft, stroke your own arm, smell the air. Panic attacks can make you feel very far away from your own body – try and reconnect with it.

- Talk to someone – make eye contact. Stroke a dog, smile at a waiter. It can help to make you see that you're not in danger. If there's nobody around, call a friend and tell them that you just need two minutes to talk – a little encouragement from my sister really helps when I'm feeling like I might have an attack.

- Expect that afterwards you're likely to feel exhausted, trembly and sometimes a little teary. The adrenaline has dissipated and your body is wrung-out. Get yourself some food, drink lots of water, sit down for a bit. Keep warm – often panic attacks leave you cold and shivery. Be nice to yourself; don't berate yourself, don't tell yourself it's pathetic. Nobody asks to have panic attacks – it's not a sign that you're weak or incapable. Tell yourself that you're OK, you handled it well, you've done well to get through it. Anxious people have minds working against them, the last thing you need is to add fuel to that.

It's important to know that while panic attacks are a beast, you will not die. They feel awful and, boy, do they take it out of you, but they cannot hurt you. Knowledge is power, and the more you understand why you've had an episode and the more you KNOW they're not dangerous, the less hold they have on you. With that in mind, it might be good to write down a bit about two times you had an attack and the events surrounding them. It's helpful to know your triggers and arm yourself with that information.

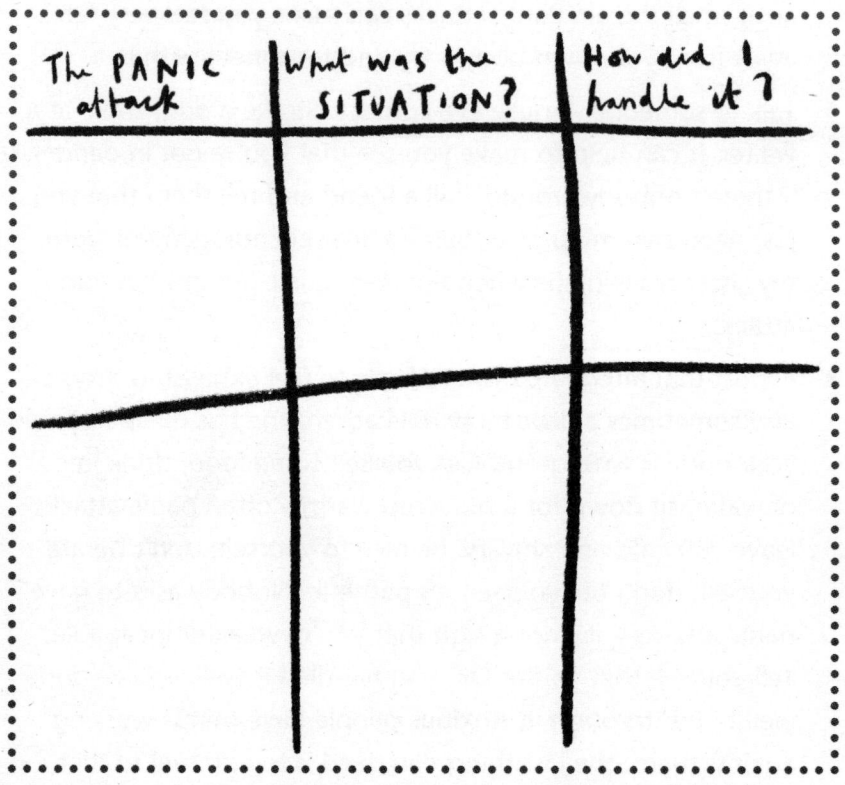

The PANIC attack	What was the SITUATION?	How did I handle it?

There are lots of ways to help prevent panic attacks – and again, you'll find your own tools. But here are a few suggestions:

Avoid caffeine – anxious people have so much adrenaline, we don't need any more encouragement.

Avoid nicotine and wine – but I guess you know this one anyway.

Try yoga/breathing exercises/ meditation – which are all known to help with stress and calm people down.

Exercise – yup hi, we've got this one covered.

Get enough sleep — sleep disturbance is often high in people with mental-health problems and it contributes to anxiety FOR REAL.[10] However you do it, make it a bigger priority.

Eat regularly. When my blood sugar drops I can feel my anxiety climbing. I try and eat every hour, which is fun and also makes me feel like a baby. Try not to forget to eat and then grab a sugary doughnut. I mean, for sure have doughnuts, but just make sure you have proper meals too.

Do things that scare you — this sounds sinister but we'll get to it and it won't sound so odd, I promise.

When a situation is looming that you find scary, plan for it. I research routes in advance so that I'll be somewhat familiar with them. I sometimes look on Google Maps and see what a venue looks like – not to plan my exit but just so I feel comfortable when I get there. This is all a way of me having an element of control over my worries. I accept I can't plan everything ahead, but I can show my anxious brain some research and say,

'Hey look! This doesn't look so bad, does it?' So much of learning to tackle anxiety is reframing your thoughts and changing the narrative in your brain. Can you start here by writing about a situation coming up soon that is making you feel a bit nervous? What would help you to stop dreading it and, if not look forward to it, then at least not let it weigh too heavily on your mind?

Future Situation | What might help make it less daunting

PART FIVE

PHYSICAL SYMPTOMS

Our minds and bodies are closely linked. Yes, that sounds mega obvious, but honestly, how often do you really take time to think about what your body might be telling your brain when it aches and feels tired? Or connect your low mood to the fact that you're getting over a bout of the flu? Yes, we all know that we're one connected being, but I think mostly we tend to view our brains as one thing and our bodies as another. I suspect many of us put our brains on a pedestal – prizing intellect – while seeing our bodies as cart horses, pulling us along. And that's not even touching on how many of us hate our bodies, see them as inferior, lacking. Too big, too short, too hairy . . .

The philosopher René Descartes proclaimed that the mind and body were two separate entities – with the mind a thinking but immaterial thing, and the body an unthinking but physical presence.* Prior to this, the mind and body were closely linked according to Christianity – and many illnesses were attributed to the victim's conduct, explained away with the notion that the person must have 'sinned'.[11] This meant that for the soul to ascend to heaven, the human body had to be intact. So theories like that of Descartes helped pave the way for medical innovation, but dismissed the bearing that the mind and body have on each other.

Nowadays, medical professionals increasingly approach treatment in a more integrated way.[12] GPs offer advice on exercise for a range of health problems and in some cases cancer patients are offered yoga and meditation to help cope with their treatment. Some surgeons even compile playlists for operating theatres, based on research that suggests that music can help reduce pain before, during and after a procedure.[13]

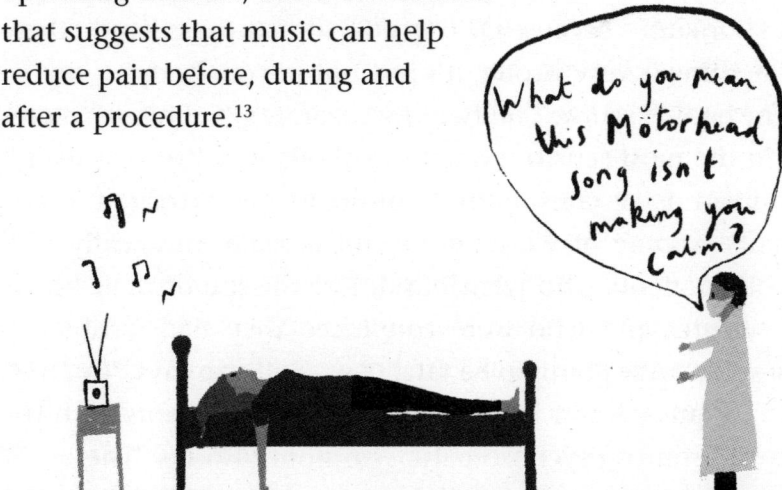

---

* I studied philosophy for about five minutes at university before anxiety overwhelmed me and I had to drop out. Probably for the best.

And yet Descartes' philosophy still holds a grip on some of us. In extreme cases, people take pills for their mind, go to the gym to hone their body – or worse, sit inert – and never connect the dots. I didn't, not for thirty years of my life. Many people with anxiety become huge hypochondriacs (ME!) and STILL don't link up their aches and pains with their mental health.

Online forums are full of scared people talking about twitchy feet and pins and needles and back ache and nausea and stomach upsets. But OF COURSE our bodies are influenced by our minds. The mind is a powerful thing. It can make you feel cripplingly ill without anything being actually wrong. Except that's bunkum – because OF COURSE something is wrong there – something is very wrong, it's just not in your body.

The book *It's All in Your Head* by Suzanne O'Sullivan explores this in the most sensitive and empathetic way I've ever read.[14] O'Sullivan is a consultant neurologist, and treated many patients – some of whom were not actually physically ill.[15] She had patients who went blind, lost the use of their limbs, had seizures and who were convinced they had terrible illnesses that were going to be fatal. As O'Sullivan says, 'In 2011, three GP practices in London identified 227 patients with the severest form of psychosomatic symptom disorder. These 227 constituted just 1 per cent of those practice populations – but estimates suggest up to 30 per cent of GP encounters every day are with patients who have a less severe form of the illness. If psychosomatic symptoms are so ubiquitous, why are we so ill equipped to deal with them?'

O'Sullivan treated these patients as seriously as she did those with more tangible illnesses. But many people, upon being told that they had a psychosomatic illness, were affronted, dismayed, in denial, and unwilling to believe it. They felt as though they were being accused of faking a problem, which is not the case at all. Their problems were as real as those of other patients. But the root cause was different.

I've felt like that, to a lesser extent. Affronted when GPs haven't taken my low blood sugar seriously. Confused when migraines were put down to anxiety and not a brain tumour as I was convinced. My low energy was tested, and my insomnia discussed, but suggestions that I might be feeling things that weren't 'real' was very upsetting. Why? Why would a mental-health issue feel less valid to many of us than a broken leg, say? Partly it's the stigma, isn't it? That a broken leg feels serious, totally genuine, more worthy of sympathy – a mental illness might be weak, or seen as our fault, or dismissed as attention-seeking.

Well balls to that. We need to start being comfortable with mental illness being just as worthy of help and attention as anything else. But in order to do that, we need to understand how deeply our minds can affect our bodies. As I've said, the first time people have a panic attack, they often don't know what on earth is going on and think they're dying. This is a common example, but it's far from the only time that anxiety will show itself physically, and it can be really terrifying.

Repeat after Me...
MENTAL HEALTH ISSUES ARE AS VALID AS EVERY OTHER HEALTH ISSUE

Aside from the host of ways anxiety has messed with my mind, it's also done a number on my body. This is not a comprehensive list BY ANY MEANS, but here's a list off the top of my head:

- Made my eyelid droop and flicker (I thought it was a stroke).
- Given me rashes, psoriasis and weird red blotches all over my body.
- Made my hair thin.
- Given me tension migraines that lasted for days.
- Made me vomit.

- Made my whole body shake so wildly I thought I was going to die.

- Given me stabbing pains in my chest.

- Made my back ache so much that moving was difficult.

- Made me feel as though my limbs were detached from me (that one is weird).

- Made my vision blurry.

- Made me so tired I found it hard to move.

- Made me lose my memory. Seriously – anxiety can mess with MEMORY.

These things were all very real to me. Not made-up, not fake, not attention-seeking. That's how strong the mind is. There's a list floating around the internet that I stumbled upon a few years back called something like '100 anxiety symptoms' and I ticked ALL of them off. It was such a relief to realise that these physical issues could be explained – and a relief to know that I wasn't alone in dealing with them.

I'm not suggesting that you chalk up all physical ailments to anxiety and never get medical help (norovirus is not all in your head). I am saying that we should all stop and think when we feel a niggle, a pain, a tingle and ask ourselves how our anxiety level is. That isn't about minimising the physical discomfort or pain we're in, it's about taking our mental health seriously and connecting the dots. So here are two little exercises to help unite the mind and body a little more.

Write down all the physical symptoms of anxiety that you've experienced, heard about or googled (you know you've googled symptoms, don't lie to this journal). Can be big or small. I'll start with a common one.

All the physical symptoms I've felt

OK, keep that list to hand, add to it when you experience a new symptom – get familiar with the way anxiety manifests itself in your body.

Now make a note of a situation when you felt ill, 'off', wrong or rundown. Think about what was going on that day – were you worried about work? Were you having anxiety attacks a lot in that period? No need to be Sherlock Holmes – just jot down anything that comes to mind.

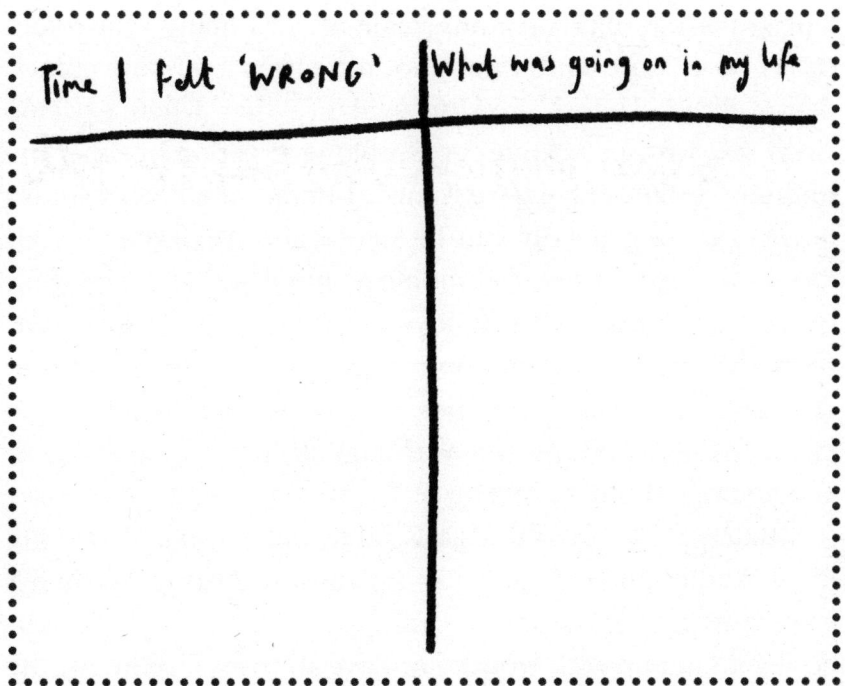

Time I felt 'WRONG' | What was going on in my life

As I said, the impact of anxiety on our bodies is very real. It might all stem from your mind, but an upset stomach is undeniably rubbish. Headaches can knock you out all day. Vomiting can force you to leave important work events. Mental-health-related issues account for the majority of sick days taken at work, and we're often more likely to tell an employer that we've got flu than to explain that our bodies have been taken over by worry.[16]

Anxiety can make it feel as though your body is breaking down sometimes. Night sweats, exhaustion, cold chills (I used to have to blow-dry my feet before I could sleep sometimes) and a propensity to pick up colds made me feel many years older than I was. Those colds might not have been a random coincidence either. There's growing evidence that when extreme stress and worry continue for a prolonged period of time, the immune system may be weakened.[17] In fact the health consequences more generally can be significant. Anxiety has been linked to heart disease, respiratory problems and digestion issues.[18] I say this not to freak you out (please don't freak out, I'll have to give my book money back) but to show you that your anxiety is SERIOUS and VALID and you deserve to be taken seriously and not feel as though it's not important. It is, and you're not 'imagining' it.

Anxiety makes our minds miserable, but it also makes living in our bodies uncomfortable and painful and tiring. So there's even more reason to make changes and seek help – you might be able to put up with worries, or have all the symptoms of the flu, but both at the same time is more than one person should have to tolerate.

And the great thing is, the more you understand the ways that your mind and body impact on each other, the more you can break the cycle of anxious thought – adrenaline – more anxiety. There's nothing radical to suggest here – no potions or expensive equipment to buy. It's the old classics as usual – sleep, exercise, good nutrition, training your brain to look at things differently (learning to reframe negative thoughts), and listening to what your body needs. Are you full of nervous energy? Maybe a walk would help dissipate some of that. Feeling cold and shaky? Have a hot bath. I hope these suggestions don't sound too like Pippa Middleton's party manual ('consider a cake', etc.). They can feel obvious but, unfortunately, there's no quick remedy which fixes all of these physical things. There's a reason the suggestions given by professionals all tend to be framed around exercise and wellbeing – it's because they work. And the more you look after your body, the less the symptoms will invade on a daily basis. Since I started running five years ago, I'm ill much less. I sleep better. I don't feel overwhelmed with adrenaline and I don't have so many weird and frightening body niggles which used to send me straight to Google to see if it meant I had cancer.

'Googling health worries online always leads to a result that says CANCER'

(An update on the saying that all roads lead to Rome)

Write down five things you know help with physical symptoms of anxiety:

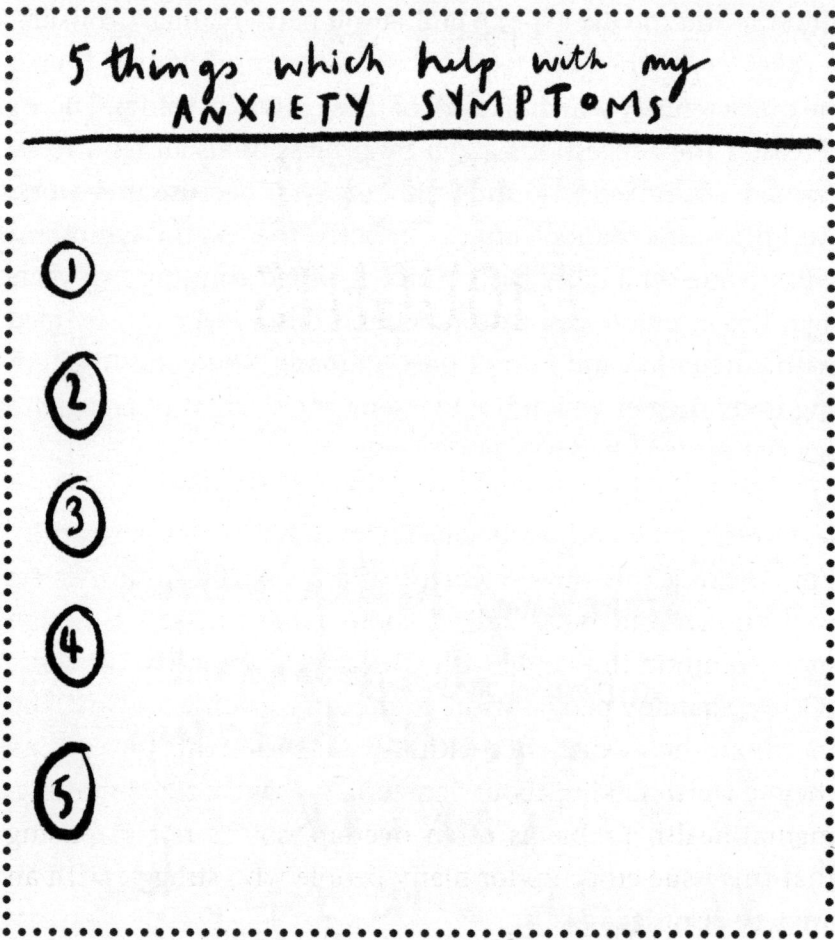

Try to do at least one a day for a week and see if you feel differently.

PART SIX

INTRUSIVE THOUGHTS

I'm covering this nasty element of anxiety even though it's less well known and rarely talked about. No, let me start again. I'm covering this nasty element of anxiety BECAUSE it's less well known and rarely talked about. That's better. Although most common in people with Obsessive Compulsive Disorder (OCD), so many people wrote to me after reading *Jog On* to tell me about their experience with intrusive thoughts that I think they're worth talking about here too. As I said at the beginning, mental-health problems often overlap, so it's not surprising that this issue crops up for many people who struggle with an anxiety disorder.

Right. Intrusive thoughts. Obsessional thoughts. Horrible thoughts. We all have horrible thoughts from time to time. The classic example often given is when standing on a station platform and suddenly looking at the person in front of you and thinking: 'I could push that man onto the train tracks.' Obviously you never would! The thought is ridiculous, stupid, weird and you shake your head, laugh, and shove it out of your mind.

OR DO YOU? For some people, that thought is horrifying, disturbing, and feels like it must say something about who you are as a person. Do you want to push someone in front of a train? Why would you do such a dreadful thing? What does that thought mean? And over and over your brain whirs, trying to figure out why that random notion popped into your mind. You try and untangle it, arguing with the thought, trying to shut it up. But it strengthens and mutates, growing other branches – 'What if you pushed a man off a platform and just don't know that you did?'

You are exhausted trying to engage and neutralise this thought. Your brain cannot think of anything else. It sets off a spiral of anxiety and despair and terror. Some people can shrug off an intrusive thought, and some of us are really susceptible to them. The thoughts become an obsession, and you cannot shake them off.

I wrote about mine in *Jog On*. It was the hardest bit to write, because these thoughts are often so weird and alien. And because, as I said, we still don't talk about them enough. If you've read *Jog On*, you know mine focused on going mad. That thought gripped me one day, and locked onto me with a vice-like grip. From there, this type of thought bombarded my brain – one would give rise to another. 'Am I going mad' would lead to 'Do I think my parents want to kill me?' which would lead to 'Oh my God, I DO think my parents want to kill me, will I have to live in a hospital?' Everything felt terrifying and strange and wrong, so my physical anxiety kicked in, geeing up these thoughts, until I was questioning the universe, wondering if life was a simulation, and on and on and on. It was the darkest period of my life. And I don't say that lightly. My every waking minute was just scary thoughts bashing against my skull (not a scientific term, obviously) and I couldn't go on like that.

Phew. I still find this stuff so hard to talk about. But I'm trying to lead from the front, and be honest about all of my weirdest anxiety stuff so that, one day, it's as boring and mundane as telling someone about your dreams (don't do that, it's never interesting).

Whether your thoughts centre around stabbing a child, or being a paedophile, or going and pushing people off station platforms, it's important to say that the likelihood that you'll ever act on those thoughts is SO LOW. A common misconception is that these thoughts mean you secretly believe them – NO! It's the opposite, if anything. They don't signify anything at all, though I know that doesn't mean a thing when you're suffering with them.

Our brains create tons of new thoughts every minute of the day. Most whizz by, we don't give them all equal significance. But these distressing ones 'stick' in our minds. And the more we argue with them, the more they embed and the 'stickier' they become.

There are common themes to intrusive thoughts – but don't worry if yours isn't mentioned – my specific one isn't found in OCD books or online very much (remember, don't google!) but it's still valid.

• Violent intrusive thoughts and/or images – this type of thought can make you worry you're a violent or bad person.

- Blasphemous thoughts – can make you worry that you're disobeying your religion.
- Thoughts questioning your relationship – this one crops up a lot and can make people doubt whether a relationship is right.
- Sexual intrusive thoughts or images – you might worry you're a paedophile or a rapist.

This unlucky affliction SUCKS, and if you suffer from it too, then let me give you a wordy hug. Can you write down some thoughts that stick in your mind? Often they are so scary that people don't ever speak them out loud for fear of making them more valid. But treating them with kid gloves gives them a level of respect they don't deserve. I've just told you my weird ones – and it feels good. Lighter even. They don't mean anything, so why not put them on paper and shrug off some of their weight?

INTRUSIVE THOUGHTS

Just to emphasise that we have lots of rubbish thoughts, can you write down a few really weird thoughts you've had in your life that DIDN'T scare you – maybe they made you laugh, or think that you're some kind of weird genius. As an example, I once wondered if the mugs in my cupboard minded being upside down, which is RIDICULOUS – but didn't become an obsessional thought. I laughed and forgot about it. Just today, I felt irrationally angry at a bad driver and wondered whether I could bumper his car. I never would! And I know that – it didn't distress me, I just drove off calmly.

List some :WEIRD: thoughts you've laughed off

Now look back at the thoughts you've just written down. The value of those thoughts is precisely nothing. They didn't upset you. You know that they didn't have any significance.

Do you see that intrusive thoughts are exactly the same now? Your thoughts are not YOU. Bad thoughts do not make you a bad person; they distress you for sure, but they don't say anything about who you are.

There are many suggestions as to how to tackle distressing thoughts. Not all of them are helpful (don't wear an elastic band on your wrist and snap it when you have a thought – I tried it, total balls). I found cognitive behavioural therapy to be amazingly helpful for reframing these kind of thoughts – find out more from your GP. Medication can really help too (more on both of these later). Some other tactics to try:

Do:

✓ Recognise these thoughts as 'intrusive'.

✓ Remind yourself that thoughts come and go – you didn't invite them in.

✓ Allow the thoughts to come into your mind. Trying to push them away increases anxiety.

✓ Try and carry on with your day while waiting for the thought to pass – hard to do, I know, but you mustn't stop your life to engage with them.

✓ Allow them to pass through your mind.

✓ Greet them light-heartedly to take away the seriousness – I sometimes say: 'Ah hello, there you are back again, blah blah.'

Don't:

X Engage with the thoughts – again, so hard not to, but it gives them a validity they don't deserve.

X Argue with them – again, they don't mean anything. It's like arguing with a toddler about philosophy.

X Push the thoughts out of your mind.

X Try and neutralise them with compulsions (repeatedly washing your hands, etc.).

X Try to figure out what your thought says about you – it doesn't say anything apart from telling you that you're feeling anxious.

This all feels very hard to do when the thoughts are flaring up. In the spirit of honesty, I needed medication to lessen the distress before I was able to utilise these techniques, so please don't feel like you're failing if you need a bit more help to combat them. It's so hard to not trust everything that your brain is telling you – but sometimes our brains are spouting bollocks. The trick is to separate out the valid thoughts from the erroneous ones. That's a hard task, but don't despair. Over time, it IS possible to see the intrusive thoughts hove into view and just think, 'Not today Satan.'

The last anxiety thing I'm going to mention is dissociation. It's common in anxiety disorders and it's not talked

- Not all thoughts mean something

- You do not have to engage with them

- Sometimes your brain is just being a dick

about enough or understood widely. The reason I know this is because of the volume of people who've been in touch with me since *Jog On* to tell me that they've suffered with it for years but never knew it had a name, or that other people experienced it. I was dumbfounded that so many people struggled with it in silence, and have vowed to yell about it whenever I can. And I'm starting here.

Dissociation can occur in many forms, and is often incredibly distressing and weird. It's thought to happen sometimes when your brain is overloaded with anxiety or trauma – a well-meaning but horrible self-preservation technique. It can be a symptom of anxiety, PTSD, schizophrenia, depression or bipolar disorder. Now is the difficult bit where I try and explain it . . .

When it's a result of an anxiety disorder, it commonly occurs in two ways:

- **Depersonalisation** – a feeling that you are watching the world without being fully part of it. You may feel detached from yourself, emotionless, as though you're observing yourself. Some people even find that their bodies feel odd, the world may feel flat or two-dimensional, and you can feel separate from it.

- **Derealisation** – a feeling of unreality, as though the world is a film set, and the people around you are actors (even though you know they're not). Things can feel grey and dreamlike.

I've had both, but really struggled with derealisation – it made me think I was losing my mind, I lived in *The Truman Show*, that I would never get back through the looking glass, and the more you worry about it, the longer it stays. What a fucker.

These episodes can last minutes, or hours, sometimes for a long period of time when you're under increased stress or feeling very depressed. There's no specific medication available, but I found that taking antidepressants lessened the frequency of the spacey moments, and CBT helped me understand why it was happening. When I feel it coming on now, I exercise. It connects me back to my body and distracts me from my own mind. I'm detailing this strange element of anxiety because I'm willing to bet that some of you are reading this and nodding along with the above symptoms.

Repeat after me:

I am not 'crazy'.
It won't last forever.
My mind is trying to protect me.

If you think you've experienced either derealisation or depersonalisation, write down what was going on at that time in your life – any stresses, illness, big life events occurring that you might not have connected to the feelings that you were having:

Times you felt disconnected

What was going on in your life?

Alongside talking therapies, there are some techniques which might help.

- Keeping a journal – it can show you triggers that might bring on an episode and help you to recognise any upcoming times which could usher in a period of dissociation.

- Tell yourself that you're safe and the feeling is temporary. I imagine I'm in my favourite garden on holiday when it hits, just to calm myself down.

- Connect with the things around you – feel different textures, taste things, smell your favourite scent. This can help ground you back in reality.

- Socialise – you don't have to go to a party, but make sure you keep seeing people; not focusing on your own thoughts can help the moment pass.

- Go for a walk – really notice where you are and what's going on in the world around you.

- Breathe deeply – this is calming, telling your body that there's no need to panic.

PART SEVEN

BAD COPING SKILLS

Right. I am good at this bit because I spent twenty years with fucking TERRIBLE COPING SKILLS. Or maybe I just didn't have any coping skills. And guess what? My mental health got worse and worse as a result. That's what happens with mental illness – leave it untreated and it gets worse, almost without exception.

Anxiety is like my new rescue dog – responds very well to training treats, responds very badly to being ignored. Excuse the tortured analogy, it's just all I've done for four months is train a dog. I have nightmares about forgetting his lead and I sometimes stare at him when he sleeps. You're lucky this book isn't 80 per cent dog content. ANYWAY.

People with mental-health issues often wait a long time before seeking help. As I mentioned earlier, this can be for a number of reasons:

- Not realising that they have a mental-health problem.
- Thinking they can cope alone.
- Hoping the problem will go away.
- Feeling embarrassed or ashamed.

This reluctance is why people go on to develop bad coping skills. Bad coping skills (often called maladaptive coping) often feel like they're helping in the short term – but they actually serve to make mental-health issues worse as time goes on. I'll give you an example from my life. When I was little, I started to develop signs of obsessive compulsive disorder. I didn't know that of course, but I knew that my family might die if I didn't flick light switches a certain number of times, or blink when I had a bad thought. These things brought me mild relief in the immediate moment, but got more and more detailed and complicated as I got older. Until I was thirty-three, I had to name the members of an old friend's family every time I brushed my teeth.

I chanted, 'Sarah, John, Marie, Andrew' every damn time. It was pointless and stupid and didn't offset my actual anxiety. That was pretty harmless, but I had tons of these made-up rules to combat the thoughts – and they ruled my life.

Reading that, I bet you can see that these mechanisms didn't help me. It's pretty obvious, huh? The small relief you get from these behaviours doesn't last – so you ramp it up, do them more frequently, or add new ones. And they lose their instant relief powers pretty quickly too.

I'm going to list some common bad coping skills here. You might recognise some of them, even if you'd not consciously realised you were doing them.

- Avoiding scenarios that make you anxious (as discussed earlier – like if you have a panic attack in a cinema and avoid cinemas).

- Compulsions – neutralising a bad thought or worry with an action (like washing your hands when you think about your parents dying).

- Relying on crutches – be that smoking, alcohol, too much coffee or junk food. I've used all of these, if it makes you feel better.

- Seeking reassurance – I've just told you something to feel better, but seeking reassurance is a cycle which only brings relief for a few minutes, before you look for it in another way.

- Not doing the things that scare you – similar to avoiding scenarios. You're scared of heights, so you don't climb that hill. But then the hill possesses a power it doesn't merit and becomes a scary figure in your mind.

* Staying hypervigilant – anxiety makes you stay on alert, and we often think that looking for exits and trying to spot signs of danger will help us prepare for the worst but it actually keeps our brain in the fight-or-flight mode.

You know what I'm going to do now, don't you? Yup, I'm going to ask you to write down any coping skills you think might be

My 'BAD' coping skills

false friends. They might not be on the list above – you might sleep too late every day to avoid facing your anxious brain, or tidy your house to excess in order to feel like you're in control of something. Whatever it is, write it down and explain to yourself why you think it helps and then honestly weigh up whether it actually does, or whether it's actually locking you into an anxious cycle – where the behaviour reinforces the problem.

I'm going to give you another example from my own life – sharing is caring and, weirdly, the more I write about my own shit, the lighter I feel. Hey, it's my journal too, right?

When I was twenty-eight I became obsessed with the idea of anaphylactic shock – the result of the immune system over-reacting to a trigger (like an allergy).[19] I must have read about a case of it in the media, and it sounded awful and scary, and somehow I got it into my brain that I might develop it. Sometimes this stuff is rooted in a past experience which your brain connects to – however weak the link is. I've had mild allergic reactions to things in the past – a weird flare-up from peach skin aged three has stuck with me ever since – so I joined the dots and came up with a bloody Jackson Pollock painting in my head. That one thought meant that I stopped dyeing my hair (and looked bloody dreadful for two years). I thought that was sensible, right? Just a little precaution, no bother. Except that avoidance reinforced the danger in my mind. So I stopped eating food I'd not had before. And I didn't use beauty products that weren't already in my cabinet. And then I stopped wearing perfume. Again, these weren't HUGE restraints on my life.

But my brain took all this as a sign of DANGER and looked for more potential risks. So I didn't want to go anywhere remote – what if I couldn't get to help? And then I started only booking trips if there was a hospital nearby (I cannot believe I'm admitting all this). And then, *voilà*, my life was impacted properly. Before I'd even realised what was happening. That's avoidance. My brain had 'learnt' that avoidance was an effective coping strategy (because it meant less immediate anxiety). So every time I had a similar worry about allergies, I used the same avoidance method. Short term, this lessened the worry, but in the long term it meant I never truly tackled the fear. Avoidance means that you don't learn that your fears are unwarranted – and really, that's the only way to kill off a specific fear effectively. As you see, that coping skill was beyond rubbish. I just felt more scared, more boxed in, more certain of impending danger. And if this all sounds too bleak, don't worry, I WILL go on to show how I put this right in the next part of this book . . .

THE GOOD BIT!

PART EIGHT

GOOD COPING SKILLS

This part is thankfully more positive. As discussed, there are MANY bad ways to deal with anxiety. Let's not lose hope, let's discuss the helpful ways to tackle it instead. I'm going to give you the main ones that have helped me, and that are also recommended by professionals (remember – me = not a professional at anything). We'll start with the help you can get from other people, and then look at the stuff you can do for yourself. Onwards!

GUIDED SELF-HELP

This is a fairly new approach from the NHS. (And is much cheaper than individual counselling. GOVERNMENT! – increase the amount spent on mental health!) You can refer yourself, or your GP can suggest a programme (online or with a textbook) which can help you work through some of your issues.[20] The NHS says that for some people, guided self-help can be just as effective as face-to-face therapy for depression, anxiety and some other mental-health issues.[21] It might also be a good place to start if you're intimidated by group therapy, nervous about one-on-one therapy, live in a remote place, or have a very busy life and not much time to spare. It's also a good starting point – if it doesn't seem like it's working for you, the NHS can refer you to other services.

TALKING THERAPIES

This is a fancy way of saying . . . well . . . therapy. There are a ton of different types of therapists and analysts available (I swear there's a comedy to be made about the professional rivalry between a Jungian and a Kleinian, but I digress) and if your local NHS service has a long waiting list, then the mental-health charity MIND has a BRILLIANT section on how else to seek help. It offers advice on where to seek reputable help, signposts those places that offer counselling on a sliding scale of cost (private therapy can be expensive) and alerts you to charities and organisations that might be able to help you with some treatment. I urge you to check it out.

The British Association for Behavioural & Cognitive Psycho-therapies (BABCP) also has a good web page listing all their members practising in your area – http://www.cbtregisteruk.com

The most frequently recommended talking therapy for anxiety disorders is cognitive behavioural therapy (CBT). It's worth noting that it focuses on the here and now, so if your issues stem from a problem in your childhood, or a trauma that you feel you need to explore, then another type of talking therapy might be better for you. I've tried several (MANY) different types of therapy and this is the one that really worked for me. CBT is based on the notion that thoughts, feelings and our physical body are all connected. If a person feels anxious or panicked, they will often fall into patterns of negative thinking, and respond to these feelings in an unhelpful way, creating a cycle which can feel hard to break out of. CBT helps you to notice these ways of thinking, and shows you how to change your behaviour.

My therapist (Hi Barry!) gave me homework at my first CBT session, which seemed unfair since school was so long ago and I hated it, but my goodness was it helpful. I realised that it was no good just expecting forty-five minutes offloading to a therapist to fix me until my next session, I had to put in some work myself. Anxiety often means seeking reassurance, and therapy can become a way of doing that (although a good practitioner won't indulge it), so knowing that you have to train your own brain can feel a bit daunting. This is the homework sheet that helped me the most. I'd like you to try it. I took home about twenty copies of this one exercise after my first session and filled one out a day. It lessened over time, but I still do it in my mind now when I feel anxious, and the aim is that it becomes your new normal way of thinking. So if you find it helps, maybe write it out yourself and do it for a few days or weeks – as long as it helps to actually write it down and not just say it to yourself.

THE WORRY	THE OUTCOME YOU ENVISAGE	THE MORE REALISTIC OUTCOME

One of my sheets looked like this:

THE WORRY	THE OUTCOME YOU ENVISAGE	THE MORE REALISTIC OUTCOME
FLYING ON A PLANE! It looks terrifying and I can't do it	The plane will CRASH and I'll plunge to my death	Planes are the safest way to travel. I'll feel anxious but I'll land safely and have a lovely holiday

Once I'd written it all down, and read it back, I went on to write down how I felt now, as opposed to how I felt at the beginning of the exercise.

So while I might have felt VERY worried at the first outcome I wrote down, I felt mild apprehension at the second, which is a pretty good result. How do you feel after looking at the more realistic outcome you wrote down? Do you see how different it is from your initial, catastrophic one? Does that make you feel a bit calmer? Try reassessing your worry and writing down how anxious you felt at the end of the exercise too. It's OK if you still feel anxious, it's just a first attempt.

INITIAL ANXIETY   ANXIETY NOW

Another really good exercise is to notice when and why you feel peaks of anxiety or low mood during the day/week/month. This guides you to understand what might be triggering you, and help you to change your behaviour or routine in order to ease the worry.

A couple of examples. Anxiety is often worse for many people in the morning. Have you ever woken up with a whoosh of adrenaline whirling in your stomach, and a feeling of dread rushing in? It's a horrible way to start the day – and I used to experience it every morning. I started to note that down, and realised a few things. Firstly, I recognised that I was hungry – low blood sugar always makes me ANXIOUS AND SAD. So

toast was added into my routine. I also realised that getting active quickly after springing out of bed was a really good way to negate some of that adrenaline, so now I try to walk or run within thirty minutes of waking up.

Some tips for dealing with anxiety in the mornings that have worked for me:

- Don't pick up your phone straight away – try and have twenty minutes without the stress of technology.

- Do some deep breathing in bed for a few minutes before you get up.

- Think of one good thing happening that you can look forward to.

- Stretch when you get out of bed – it can help release some of those nervous initial feelings.

- Eat something sharpish – your blood sugar is low and that makes us feel more anxious.

Another thing that really hypes my worry up is premenstrual syndrome.[22] Just before I get my period, my anxiety levels are much higher and my mood is much lower. What a combination, huh? Again, I wrote this down, and assessed what, if anything, helped this time in the month. I tried a new vitamin, taking an iron supplement, sleeping a bit more and, importantly, learning not to worry about the worry. I would tell myself that it was PMS, not a creeping breakdown approaching, and that it would pass. And that really helps me now. By writing it down – I made the connection between situational anxiety and the way I could take steps to reduce it. Sometimes just knowing what the underlying factor is can really help. Say it with me:

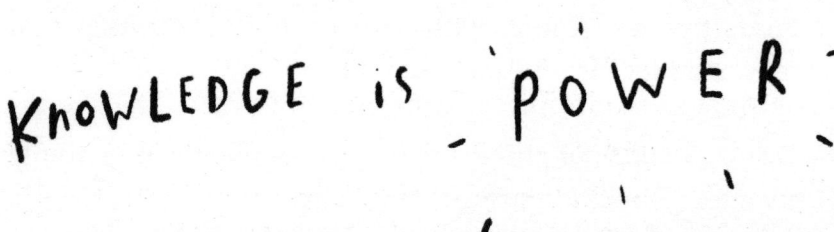

KnoWLEDGE iS POWER

Write down a few examples for yourself, and come up with a few ideas to help these periods of anxiety or low mood that you encounter regularly. Note down how implementing those ideas makes you feel next time you are hungover, or worried about a weekly meeting, or anxious on a Sunday night (I know that one's not just me).

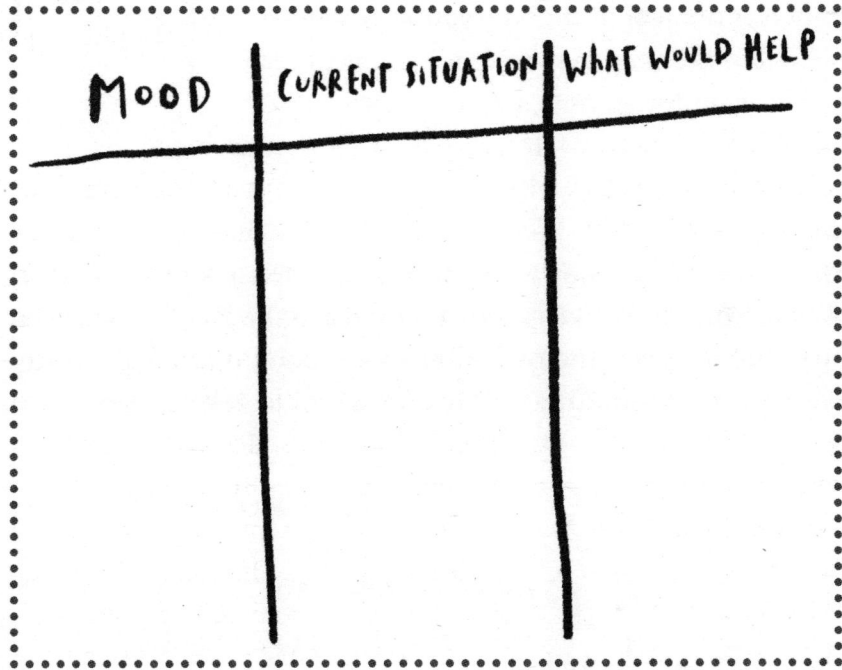

CBT is structured, requires a lot of work outside of sessions, and involves confronting your emotions and challenging thoughts. It's not easy, but I'd really recommend it. Your GP will be able to give you information about how to go about it, and the MIND website has lots of facts about it too.

MEDICATION

I talk about medication at length in *Jog On* and I don't want to repeat myself too much, but it's important to reiterate a few things. I got lots of messages from readers who told me that they were reluctant to take medication for anxiety, OCD or depression because it somehow felt 'weak' or they were worried about 'failing to deal with it by themselves'. Other people were too embarrassed to take it in case loved ones or colleagues thought it meant they were 'crazy', and a few people were even worried that it would stultify them, leave them emotionless or spaced out. It was the one thing in the book that people really were fearful of, and that made me sad. So let me just say:

MILLIONS of people take medication for their mental health, sporting heros, actors, scientists, politicians - that aunt your mum hates. that cousin you love, that funny. brilliant friend you don't see enough. And some dogs too.

I'm not even joking about the dogs by the way.[23] There were more than 70 million prescriptions for antidepressants in England in 2018, so this isn't some tiny group of people who all live in one village and have worse mental health than you.[24] That would be weird, for sure. We need to talk about our usage of them more so that all the people who got in touch with me who needed help but were scared of medication could feel like they weren't having to make this choice alone.

And it is a choice – you don't have to take medication if you don't want to. Lots of people choose to cope with mental-health issues without it, but lots of people really need meds in order to live their lives. Educate yourself about what medication would really look like for you – not what some tabloid newspaper says, or what the office bore claims. Talk to your GP, or to a mental-health charity. If you have a loved one who's taken them, have a conversation about how they found the process.

I found them a lifesaver – at moments when I was a tearful, panicky, desperately sad person with no hope, they lifted my mood and helped shake off the worst of my anxiety so that I could get to a point where I could see a better future and start making some positive changes (I sound like Mr Motivator). I had a few side effects – like night sweats – but nothing like the horror stories you hear sometimes. And withdrawal can be really hard, for sure, but again, with proper research and support, it can be done. It might also be helpful to write down a list of the reasons that medication scares you, or makes you hesitant. Talk through those fears with your GP or a mental-health professional. I'm not urging you to take medication, or telling you it's the only path – far from it – but some people struggle on when they really could benefit and I just really want people to know that SO MANY AMAZING PEOPLE TAKE something for their mental health and they aren't weak, or failing, or emotionally numb.

Jim Carrey!
Jon Hamm!
Amanda Seyfried!
Kristen Bell!
Chrissy Teigen!
(This was just a quick google of names you might know.)

This is an Orthopedic Boot. You'd wear one for a broken ankle wouldn't you?

This is medication for blood pressure. You'd take that if you needed it wouldn't you?

BLOOD PRESSURE

The brain is a part of you. If something's not working well, there's medication that can help – just as there is if you have the flu, or need antibiotics. I really believe that if we start seeing mental-health meds as normally as we would prescriptions for physical ailments, that would go some way to reducing the shame and stigma that still surround them.

MEDITATION AND MINDFULNESS

These practices can help you learn how to allow thoughts to come and go without engaging with them, master breathing exercises which help to lessen physical symptoms of anxiety, and manage worry. There is good evidence of their effectiveness for several mental-health issues (anxiety being one) and the great news is that you don't need a referral or a costly teacher to begin either.[25] There are tons of meditation exercises online, and lots of books about mindfulness to get you started. Many people use apps now to guide them through mindfulness and breathing sessions. I use breathing techniques when I'm feeling particularly overwhelmed or having a hard time getting to sleep, and they never fail to calm me down. I focus on taking a deep breath (feeling it in my stomach and not just my chest) and pay attention as I exhale. And I keep on doing that for as long as I need – letting thoughts flow in and out, but refocusing my attention on my breathing. It's very helpful for learning how not to label thoughts as good or bad, but just to know that they'll wander away if you choose not to engage. If you use these techniques enough, you can employ them in stressful situations to help lower your anxiety levels.

Try a breathing exercise for five minutes when you're feeling stressed out. Sit down somewhere comfortable and close your eyes if it feels nice. Relax your body so that your shoulders drop, your arms are loose and your feet are flat on the floor, legs slightly apart. Breathe in through your nose, feeling your stomach extend, and try to do this for five seconds. Breathe out through your mouth, feeling your belly empty. Repeat slowly, and feel your muscles relax. Focus on steady breathing, and try not to follow any one thought too far down the tracks. See how you feel afterwards – the more you practise this, the more you'll be able to contain anxious moments in the future.

HOBBIES

At the risk of sounding like your mother (no shade to your mother), I find creating stuff and using my hands really lessens anxiety. There's a reason I listed therapy and medication first, but this is a really good avenue to explore if you've tackled the worst elements of your anxiety and feel able to try a few more, shall we say, holistic approaches. 'Hobbies' might not really be the right word, but I struggled to find a pithy header here. What I really mean is finding a skill or craft that makes you happy, distracts your brain and takes you out of yourself for a bit. I first discovered this with baking – making intricate and beautiful cakes, pastries and buns focused my mind on something other than anxious thoughts for a while. Mixing, whipping, icing all required my brain to think about good smells, sensations and tastes – rather than panic, think 'what if' thoughts and imagine future worries. Art is a great example of this – drawing and painting and sculpting have been used as part of CBT treatment in studies – and focusing on the process allows people to express their emotions in a positive way.[26] There are so many outlets to choose from – gardening is one that helps many people, as are sewing and DIY. Try a few out, and get creative. Anxiety is often such a destructive thing, so it's really wonderful to channel energy into creating something and having something tangible to be proud of. Just don't worry too much about the result – it's the process that really counts, not the 'perfect' product. (I say this in case you ever see some of my cakes.)

Is it meant to look like that?

Journalling also follows this process (cough, cough) so here's the bit where you write down two hobbies you enjoy (even if you don't do them regularly). Note how they make you feel in the moment, and try and resolve to try to do them a couple of times a week – even if it's just baking a few cakes or doodling for fifteen minutes.

Hobbies I like	How do they make me feel?

'Vulnerability is the birthplace of INNOVATION, CREATIVITY and CHANGE'

Brene Brown

(ok it's sort of a motivational quote but come on. it's BRENE BROWN!)

TALK, TALK, TALK

Here I am, a stranger, talking to you about all my weird anxiety. And it has released me somewhat. I no longer have to worry about remembering who knows what about my mental health – 'My family knows nearly all of it, some friends know about the panic attacks, work know I'm a worrier, most people know nothing.' If you read *Jog On*, or caught any of the surrounding publicity, then you know I've been hobbled by mental-health issues for years. If I was online dating now, a prospective love interest could do a quick google and find out that I worried my family were aliens. And yet I no longer find that daunting. I guess in some ways I demand more from other people now – get on board with understanding mental health better or jog on. (Ha! So on brand.) I also no longer see it as a weakness, or as a shameful thing. And that's really because I have been so lucky to be surrounded by open-minded people who, if they didn't understand what I was going through, at least attempted to. I know that's not the case for many others. I've had messages from so many people who've said that they've had negative reactions from loved ones, employers and colleagues when they've attempted to talk about their mental health. Throughout history, people with mental-health issues have been shunned by society, marginalised, punished. We've made progress – great leaps forward in fact – but some people will still think you're attention-seeking, dangerous, broken. I say this to acknowledge that talking is not as easy for some as it is for others. And yet, it is so important for the sufferer to be able to open up and explain the weight of their thoughts and feelings. So where do you start?

From experience, it's good to pick a trusted friend or family member to open up to at first. Be as honest as possible, and come prepared with some information about what you're experiencing. There may be questions, or they may just listen. It's not your job to educate them on every mental-health issue – just be as open as you feel comfortable being, and hopefully they will care enough to do research in their own time and not bombard you. Have a chat when you're relaxed – The Time to Change Campaign recommends talking in a place you'd nor- mally get together with a pal or relative – over coffee, or on a walk.[27] Remember that the person listening loves you, and that you'd want to help if the situation was reversed.

If they need a bit of help understanding, or don't take it seriously at first, point them in the direction of a mental-health charity, or show them a book or an article that rings true to your experience. Above all, remind yourself why you're opening up. Talking about mental-health issues helps us feel less alone – a feeling so common in those who suffer. The amount of people who said that reading *Jog On* made them feel like they weren't the only one struggling was astounding to me – and has made me even more passionate about encouraging other people to share their experiences. You may be surprised by what others tell you if you admit that you have some anxiety or depressive episodes. A man got in touch with me after reading my book a few months back, and told me that he was struggling with depression but didn't know how to tell his wife – he was scared of letting her down. (Men are much less likely to talk about their mental-health issues – to loved ones or professionals.)[28] A few weeks later, he came back to tell me that he'd told her how he was feeling and that she'd listened, not judged him, and taken him to the GP to get some help. He said he felt intense relief and like a burden had been lifted from him. He was no longer struggling alone – and that's the most wonderful feeling. If we talk, we not only make ourselves feel better, we show others who struggle that they're not alone. I'm not saying that it's your responsibility to bat-signal to everyone else out there with mental-health issues, but the more we all feel able to talk about this stuff, the more it's normalised for us ALL. A positive cycle, as opposed to all the negative cycles I've been banging on about here. And here endeth the lecture on talking. Nope, tricked you. I want you to write some stuff down (I've been talking for too long). If you're already a veteran of talking it out with friends and loved ones, skip this bit if you want. But if you think, 'Oh maybe I've not been completely honest about what I'm dealing with' so far, then picture someone close to you, and try writing down what you'd like to say to them about your mental health. You don't have to do it today, but get a sense of what you need them to know, and also write down what you need from them in return.

Who do you want to talk to?	What would you like them to know?	What do you need them to know?

NATURE

There's a Carl Jung quote I found that really helped me when I first started running. 'Whenever we touch nature, we get clean.' I found that to be a brilliant summation of how I felt being outside when I ran, away from sterile office furniture and busy roads. I felt calmer, more 'normal', and more hopeful when I ran in the woods, or in parks, or down canals teeming with wildlife. Research backs up the mood-boosting effects of being in nature – and luckily you don't have to be halfway up an isolated mountain in order to get the benefits.[29] Even just a small patch of greenery can have a calming effect. Or cultivating a beautiful window box, or going on a walk through the local fields. One recent study showed that people who spent two hours in nature every week reported that their mental wellbeing and health was better than those who did not.[30] So get outside when you're feeling nervous, or when you can feel your mood crashing. Again, I know it's easier to curl up and hibernate, but even a fifteen-minute walk in your local park can offer a mood lift in a way that hiding away can't. If you can't get into the countryside, try eating your lunch in a park near work, or walking part of your commute (if it's scenic). The natural light you get is a massive bonus – we all spend too much time inside and forget how important sunlight is for our mental health.

Nature will give you (FOR FREE)

- SUNSHINE
- FRESH AIR
- NATURAL BEAUTY
- Colour to DAZZLE your eyes

Try and figure out how you can work your way up to two hours in nature every week. Could you force your kids out for a long walk on the weekends? Or take the dog out before work every day this week? Could you spend time gardening, even if you've got to wrap up warm? (I'm under no illusions that our British weather makes it easy to get outside every day.)

EXERCISE!

Since much of this journal is about RUNNING, I will just say here that going for a jog is not the only exercise that can help mental health. Lots of people find that swimming, boxing and yoga work wonders for their mood. Same with walking, trampolining or even jazzercise (does anyone still do that?). Running isn't for everyone, and it's completely OK if it's just not your thing. But it's important to find YOUR RUNNING. Find the movement that makes you happier, calmer, stronger. That might just be dancing in your room for fifteen minutes every morning. It might mean lifting heavy weights until you grunt like angry Hulk. It matters not what you do, it just matters that you do something.

As I've banged on about before, our minds and bodies are tightly linked, and hugely dependent on each other. Yet while we're all encouraged to use our brains as much as possible, physical exertion is often seen as a chore, as unenjoyable, something to be endured or avoided if possible. We do thirty minutes in the gym grudgingly. We find it hard to locate the motivation to get active. We all need to change our perspective on exercise. Sure, a freezing cold PE lesson at school was pretty grim for most of us, but that's not how it has to be as an adult. There are so many options these days when it comes to exercise – and so many reasons to do it. The physical benefits are well known, but for me, the mental-health wins are the most important. People think it's too easy a fix (I did too), as though exercise is something that works for others but not for them. But there's a reason it helps so many people – and it's not because they were somehow made 'sporty' and you weren't.

I fucking hate inspirational quotes as a rule (you know the ones – 'You're a diamond, don't let anyone hide your light, blah blah'), but I'm always in the mood for Richard Simmons. Remember him? The little guy with curly hair who encouraged people across America to work out in the 80s and 90s? Your mum probably had one of his videos. Google him, his story is fascinating. And I like his jazzy style.

'Number one, LIKE yourself.
Number two. you have to eat HEALTHILY.
And number three. you've got to
SQUEEZE YOUR BUNS'
Richard Simmons

Do you know how exercise can help alleviate some mental-health problems? I know you've heard people say it can – but do you know specifics? A vague notion that it's good for the mind is all well and good but it's helpful to see real-life benefits if you need more motivation to start.

- Exercise can help you sleep better. People who do thirty minutes of moderate exercise per day may find that they get to sleep quicker, and see a difference in the quality of said sleep.[31] This is important, because a lack of shut-eye can really impact your mental health.[32] I am always way more anxious if I've had a bad night's sleep, and this anxiety spike can in turn make it harder to sleep the next night. A long run in the morning really tires my body out by the time I get to bed in a way that a whole day in front of a computer screen can't.

- Exercise boosts cardiovascular health, which helps increase your energy levels. Before I started running, I was constantly exhausted – a byproduct of anxiety – and assumed exercise would make me *more* tired. But the opposite was true – so for those of you who are left zonked by mental-health problems, a walk, a swim or some gentle stretching can really make a difference to that seemingly never-ending fatigue.

- Exercise provides mood-improving hormones – most people refer to the endorphin rush (though some research suggests it's not actually endorphins and that is the limit of my scientific understanding here) – and it's my personal experience that this hormone rush is often an immediate thing after a workout. My mood improves, any grumpy thoughts are banished and I feel more positive about the day ahead.

- Exercise improves self-esteem. Why? Because you're doing something, sticking at it and improving. Mental-health problems so often leave us full of self-loathing, but being able to take up a skill and work hard at it can bring you so much pride in yourself. So many people contact me after their first 5k run to tell me that they never imagined that they could do something like that – they are bursting with a new sense of achievement, which they can build on in other areas of their lives.

- Exercise connects you with other people – a lot of activities foster a sense of community or team spirit. If you're feeling lonely or isolated, joining a gym class or a local netball team can connect you with other people and bring you back into the world a little bit. At times when I'm feeling like I've spent too much time in my own brain, I'll arrange to run with a friend and instantly feel a bit better. Parkrun is a brilliant example of this – and there's sure to be one local to you (search their website for details). Don't be put off if you're a beginner – all levels of ability are catered for!

Write down three exercises you might like to try – anything at all – and commit to trying them out over the next month. You don't have to sign up to an expensive gym or commit to a course, YouTube has thousands of free videos that offer workouts you can do in your bedroom. I like the channel Fitness Blender, which caters to beginners and those who can stand a little more high intensity.

Exercises I can try	What looks fun about them?

SECTION TWO

RUNNNNNNINNGGGGG!

PART ONE

GETTING STARTED

Here we are, anxious and ready to run. I told you, we're a niche group. I cannot teach you how to win a marathon, or beat Usain Bolt in a race. I cannot offer you deep nerdy technical running chat. That is not me. I'm faintly jealous of those people but I know that it's not how I work. What I CAN offer you is this:

- A look at why running can be so good for mental-health issues.

- A way to start and not give up when it gets hard.

- An outlook on running which hopefully means you'll find utter joy in it.

- Tips on pitfalls and disappointments.

- Pointers on developing an approach which allows you to do it in your own way.

- A look at running without comparing yourself to others.

- Practical advice.

- Some embarrassing running failures of my own.

- Dog photos (cheap and empty promise there).

The most common thing people say to me is that they'd like to run but they're crap at it. Or they're 'not a runner', as though some deity was in the delivery room, witnessed our births and immediately decided whether we were runners or decidedly NOT runners. WRONG! If you're lucky enough to have the use of your legs, you can be a runner. Get some trainers, put them on and wobble off. There – runner! There are no other qualifications here. Maybe some sports require more (I guess I couldn't just pick up a 50lb weight and magically become a weightlifter for example) but not this one. So get it out of your head that you can't. If you've attempted to run before and hated it, fear not. You might just have tried it on a bad day, or gone too fast too quickly, or thought you had to do miles in your first week. Let's reset. And for those of you starting out, shove any ideas you might have about running to the back of your mind while we look at it with fresh eyes and an open mind.

I should probably reiterate why I attribute my improved mental health to running. I've got a lovely family, I'm privil-

'The trouble with jogging is that by the time you realise you're not in shape for it, its too far to walk back'

FRANKLIN JONES

eged beyond belief in so many ways, I had access to therapy, and I took medication. Yet none of these support structures could alleviate the mental-health issues I had enough for me to live a full life – one not weighed down by fear and a sense of creeping doom. All of them helped enough for me to never stay in the ultimate pit of despair for too long (though I had many moments there), but I got to the age of thirty without ever really finding something that helped break the unrelenting anxiety wheel I'd been on for so many years.

I decided to go for a run shortly after my first husband

left me (how glamorous it is to say 'first', I feel like Elizabeth Taylor). I don't know why it was running and not, say, cycling or boxing. But I guess it's because running looked freeing, and I really hadn't felt that since I was a small child. It also looked nicely close to running away – except you come back when you feel ready. Lastly, it was something I could do alone. I'm a fairly solitary person and I like being on my own a lot. I wasn't comfortable trying to do a group activity, and running seemed like a good secret challenge.

A lot of people feel intimidated when they first start exercising.[1] We worry about people looking at us, about making a spectacle of ourselves, about not being good enough. I'm sure this partly stems from school PE classes, where the horror of being picked last for a team activity stayed with many of us well into adulthood (closely followed by the horror of being picked at all and praying you don't let your side down disgracefully).

This feeling is a hard one to overcome – and something people often share with me as their number one reason for not exercising. I felt it too at the beginning, which is why I chose to run up and down a dark alleyway at night so as not to be seen by people. I don't recommend this tactic particularly, but I think that starting off on side streets or on a quiet lane can be a good thing to do for the first few goes, just until you've got your confidence up a little.

But I'm getting ahead of myself! (I should have said running away with myself because I'm always on brand . . .) As

I said, I picked running as something to try and break myself out of misery. I had no long-term intentions, had never exercised before, and didn't really hold out much hope it would do much for me. And my first runs were all hard and miserable. But for some reason, I carried on going back to that alleyway, and running a little more each day. The changes were tiny at first – I cried a little less, I didn't feel quite so useless. And soon, the changes got more noticeable. I was able to run on more public roads without having panic attacks, I was sleeping a bit better. I felt braver. This shift happened within the first few weeks of jogging by the way, it didn't take years of relentless and unrewarding runs to see the benefits. I grew in confidence when I ran. I liked how independent I felt. I calmed down, felt less controlled by the adrenaline whooshing round my body, noticed a slow but steady sense of hope moving over me. All of these positive changes made me stick at it – and a good thing it started helping so quickly, because before I found running I was prone to quit anything I wasn't very good at. I quit a lot of things.

The discovery that running made me feel better was revelatory, given my low expectations. I decided that I would write down what I wanted from running – partly as motivation, partly because I wanted to see if my sense that running was easing my anxiety would be proved right long term. My list looked like this:

- Time away from everything

- A challenge

- To calm panic attacks

- To feel braver

- A chance to stop crying

- A way to look better

(That last one by the way . . . I'd just had a big break-up – it was that or cut my hair.)

PART TWO

GOALS

Write down why you want to run. Any reason is OK, as long as it's not 'To have a better chance at escaping from the police after I've committed terrible crimes' – I don't want to be complicit in anything. It's a good thing to have tangible goals and be able to look back at a later date and see whether running is helping you achieve them. That way, if it is, then fantastic! You'll feel like you've really gotten somewhere. And if not, you can either reconsider the goals, or think about whether running is the right way of getting to them. Starting anything without a clear idea about *why* you're doing it can mean you lose motivation. And these goals can hang out at the back of your mind when it's rainy or cold, or you're tired and feel like skipping a run.

What do I want to get from running?

Now write down just ONE goal for the first week of running (if you've run before, that's OK – this is a blank slate – so write down a goal you want from the next week of running ahead of you). Keep it simple – no 'I want to run a marathon' here please. This is a small and achievable goal that you can reach – maybe 'I'd like to run twice this week', or something less wedded to numbers, like 'I'd like to get some early morning energy' or 'I want to feel less anxious.' You can even just write down how you'd like to feel after the first few runs – 'I want to be proud of myself' is a nice one, or 'I want to have tried something out of my comfort zone.'

ONE GOAL for the first week of RUNNING!

Making a goal each week that you run is a really helpful thing to do when you're getting started. It keeps you motivated, it helps you see how you're improving and it gives you something to strive for. Please don't think that this means you have to set yourself punishing distance goals or aim for personal best times. We're running to improve our mood and lessen anxiety, and setting harsh goals often just ramps up worry. Sometimes my goal is 'Calm my brain down' if I'm having an anxious week. Sometimes it's 'Get some sunshine and see some nature' if I'm in a beautiful place. Sometimes it's just 'To be on my own for an hour.' It has been known that sometimes I run so I can have a massive ice cream when I'm finished. (You can have a massive ice cream without the run too, of course, it just feels even better when you're hot and energised.)

Running goal for
the week

End of week
observations

My goals were vague, but I found that the more I ran, the more I felt like I was achieving them. It helped that I didn't put any insistence on distance or pace for those early runs, because I might have disappointed myself that way. Instead, when I felt braver, I would run a little bit further – along a main road that might previously have made me feel panicky. Or when I realised that I had run for more than five minutes without stopping and wheezing, I'd feel more confident and that would spur me on to do five more.

I've made you write out some week-by-week goals for running. Keep doing that for as long as you need to, and come back to it if you feel yourself flagging.

Whatever your goal, remember that running:

- Gives you valuable alone time.
- Boosts the levels of several neurotransmitters that affect mood.
- Makes you feel strong.
- Connects you to the outside world.
- Gives you a new level of independence.
- Makes your brain take a backseat for a bit.
- Challenges you.
- Amps up your energy levels.

You know it can help you. Now let's talk about the confidence needed to actually get out there.

PART THREE

CONFIDENCE

As I said, I felt very self-conscious about exercise. I'm sure many of you feel the same way. So let's start with the most important lesson to learn:

NOBODY IS LOOKING AT YOU WHEN YOU RUN!

I mean it. You start off running head down, as though you're hiding from the FBI, covered head to toe in baggy clothes, and before you know it, you're joyously flailing down a hill wearing a pair of moth-eaten shorts and not much else. (This might just be me but you get the point.) People are self-centred monsters. Most of them are on their phones. If they look at you, do you know what they're thinking? It's one of two things:

That person is hurtling towards me, I better move.

Or, more likely:

God that person's going fast, I wish I could run.

And that's usually it. Think about every time you've seen someone out running. What did you think? I bet you looked at them admiringly, and thought they looked fucking brilliant just flying along the street. I bet you didn't think, 'Oh that person looks stupid, I'm so glad I don't run.' Am I right?

So banish self-conscious thoughts from your head. You're not doing this to seek approval from anyone else. You're doing this to make your head calmer, to spend some time alone, to achieve something – and no stranger on the street should come between you and that aim. The great thing about running is that anyone you pass, whether they notice you or not,

is behind you within the blink of an eye. You're ten steps gone
– you cannot be held in that moment if you don't want to be.

I know it seems hard to trust me on this, but put your faith
in me and you'll see that I'm telling you the truth when you've
been running for a few weeks.

- I run for myself

- Nobody cares what I'm doing

- Rinse and Repeat

Having the confidence to start running isn't just about
shrugging off the worry about what people think of you. It's
also adjusting your mindset about what you can do. As I mentioned, mental-health issues can leave us with really shitty
levels of self-esteem. Nobody who's experienced anxiety or
depression is likely to read this journal and think, 'Yeah I'm
going to crush this running thing.' (Probably because it's not
1988 and nobody talks like that.)

You're probably reading this thinking, 'Oh it's OK for you
and everyone else, but I'm terrible at running. I'll never be
good at it.' But here's the thing – there is no such thing as a
good runner or a bad runner. Yes, OK, if you're a professional
athlete then there is such a thing, fine you got me. But in a

world where the rest of us are amateurs and doing it to find some joy and get through the difficulties that life throws at us, there are no categories you need to strive for. Once you realise this, you're freed up to just try it. I have not improved on the time it took me to run a kilometre in FIVE years of running. This bothered me a bit at the beginning – surely the point was to improve? But the more I thought about it, the more I realised that speeding up wasn't one of my goals. Great if it is – if it's something that makes you feel good and improves your experience of running. But also totally fine if it isn't. It's OK to just *run* – and never be fast or sleek or have calves that look like they belong to a Greek god. Though that would be nice too.

If you go into running thinking that you have to be this fast, or look this way, or run for miles and miles, then you're likely to be disappointed when you can't, or don't, or it isn't enjoyable. Instead, it's better to start off by thinking, 'OK, this will be a challenge, I might find it difficult and sweaty and hard going, but that doesn't mean that I'm bad at it.' Motivation is helpful, but huge goals are not – not at the beginning anyway. And the way you talk to yourself is key here. If you tell yourself you'll be crap, you're honestly more likely to feel you've been crap. Our brains run on what we feed them. Negative thoughts encourage more negative thoughts. We pessimists say that we do it to protect ourselves from disappointment or guard against catastrophe, but those things come whether you think a certain way or not, and in the meantime, your mindset is gloomy for no good reason.

By the way, I say this as someone who is relentlessly negative and cynical. That's why I hate motivational quotes. That's why I am suspicious of overly cheerful people (what are they hiding?). But a lifetime of negative thoughts did very little for me, and if I'd maintained that way of thinking when I ran, I would've quit for sure. If you want to do it, you've got to believe that you can. Say it with me:

- I CAN run
- I CAN be good at it
- I AM a runner

OK, good. Now write down three reasons why you'll be good at it. It could be 'My legs are strong' or it might be 'I am fucking stubborn and will power on.' It can just be 'I'm fabulous so running will love me.' It doesn't matter how silly it seems, just come up with some ways that YOU can make running work.

3 reasons why I will be good at
RUNNING

①

②

③

TEN RUNNING MYTHS

Remind yourselves that these are all bollocks
whenever you need to:

1. You have to be thin.

Rubbish, lots of runners don't look like
Paula Radcliffe and they ace it nonetheless.

2. You have to race.

Nonsense. You run as far as you want to.
There's no set path.

3. You have to carb-load/eat protein bars/
drink sports drinks.

Nope. I barely look at my diet and I'm fine.
If you start doing mega-long runs, then these things
can help but don't worry about it now.

4. A slow run isn't a run.

LIES. Go at the pace which feels good.
Running fast and hating it is torture.

5. You must run every day.

Nope. Run as often as you like.
Three times a week is plenty.

6. You must rest regularly.

Yes, if you want to take a day off running, do.
If you feel like your body needs a rest, listen.
But I run when I want to. Be intuitive.

7. Don't run when it's too hot or too cold.

Oh hush. Run if it feels OK.
But don't run in ice. Not worth it!

8. Your knees/joints/face will get damaged.

Yes, runners get injuries. But all sport carries a risk
and research actually shows running can reduce the
likelihood of osteoarthritis long term.

9. You're too old/short/not the 'right body shape' for a run.

Like weight, you can run whether you're
long and flexible or short and, well, not flexible.
And age has nothing to do with anything as long
as you're healthy.

10. You must always strive to be better.

This is my worst one. You can aim for a faster run
every week if it makes you happy. But if you get to 5k
and feel like that works for you on a long-term basis,
then that's just as valid!

PART FOUR

ANXIETY AND EXERTION

Since this journal is about running primarily for mental health, let's acknowledge that a lot of people worry that exercise will make them fall over, have a panic attack, or worse.

Firstly, starting something new means change, and that can cause a spike in anxiety. Along with the normal trepidation about a new thing and not being good enough, people with mental-health issues can have extra worries. With running specifically, some will have concerns about their health, about their safety out on the streets alone, about whether they will have a panic attack in the middle of a run, or even just about being on their own.

Does anything give you concern beyond the usual 'I'm not fit enough' worries that everyone starting out with exercise feels? Write them down:

Worries about running

I faced some of these when I began running and will attempt to offer some tips and some reassurance (even though reassurance is not helpful long term – it just makes you seek more reassurance . . .).

First there's that capacity in all of us who struggle with our brains to catastrophise. So you plan a run and then worry about what might happen on it – will you get hit by a car, or have a panic attack, or faint in the middle of the road? What if you fall into the canal, or get mugged, or catcalled or . . . OMG I don't want to go now. That's how fast your mind can spiral into doom.

We can unpick some of these worries about physical sensations later on, but first let's try and challenge the worry thoughts with some more rational ones. The likelihood is, the next run you take will be hard. You'll sweat, and probably hate some of it, and maybe you'll be slow but the worst thing that will happen is that your leggings will start sagging. At the end, you'll feel proud of yourself and have a nice rewarding hot chocolate/ice cream/gluten-free muffin/glass of wine – delete as appropriate. That's it. That's all that will happen. And it's important to challenge those big fears, because otherwise you'll work yourself up and put it off and then feel scared when you should be concentrating on your new experience.

Firstly, you're not going to faint. It's SUCH a common anxiety worry, but we talked earlier about why it's not going to happen. If you feel faint, you'll remember that it's because you're pushing yourself and you're out of breath from that exertion – it's not fear, it's fitness.

You are not going to have a terrible accident. The worst thing that's happened to me while running is that I fall over a lot. I am very clumsy and stack it fairly often on runs. I get bruises and occasionally some scrapes, but I get up and carry on. Not once have I fallen into a canal, and you won't either.

You will take care to listen for traffic – running in the direction of oncoming traffic if you're on country roads and on pavements in urban areas. You'll wear bright clothing (any excuse to be jazzy) and if you're running at night in a place with bad lighting, you'll wear a head torch or lights on your shoes.

You can stop at ANY TIME if you need to – that's the joy of running. If it feels too fast, or you're getting a bit anxious, stop and walk for a few minutes. Let your heart rate return to normal and drink some water. Then check yourself – all OK? Slowly start up again.

You can stay close to home – I ran the block around my house for so long before I ventured further. And even then, I only ran around my neighbourhood for a few weeks before I had the courage to go to new places. That's fine! It's all OK – loops of a place you feel safe are completely valid and also mean you don't have to trek all the way home. Win–win.

You can prep – I'm a chaotic mess most of the time, but if I'm anxious about something new, I research and check out routes and get as much info as I can. So feel free to plot the route you'll take on initial runs, so it doesn't feel unfamiliar or scary.

OK, now write down a more rational scenario for your run:

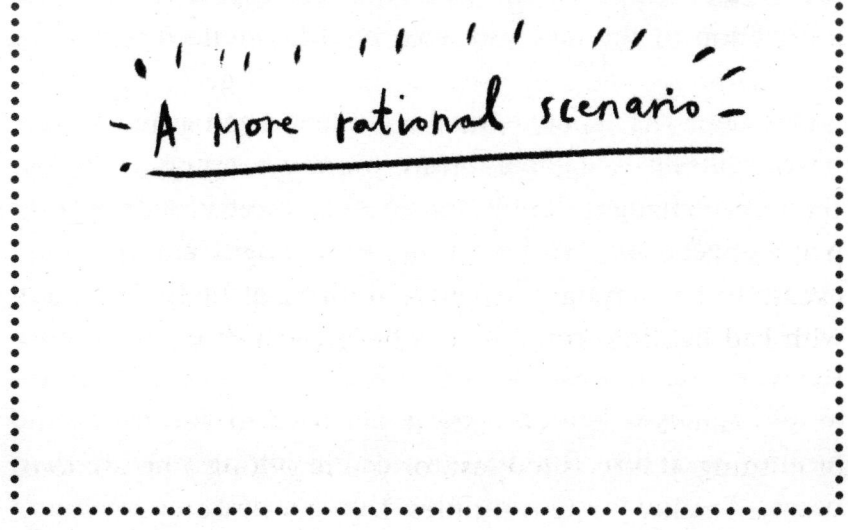

PART FIVE

PREPPING

We're confident, we don't care who sees us, we've got some motivation in the tank. So what else do we need before we run?

We need KIT. Look, when you're first starting out, I think it's completely acceptable to run in old sweatpants and those trainers you bought eight years ago when you decided you were going to get a six-pack before the summer and then promptly ate a tub of ice cream and put the trainers in the cupboard full of old blankets and that tennis racket you've not used since school (is that too specific to be anyone but me?). The big ath-leisure brands would like you to believe that you need £100 leggings and shoes that have words like 'fly' attached to their names. But the joy of running is that it's FREE and shouldn't exclude anyone because you can't afford the gear. So don't worry too much if you're just starting out. But beyond the first couple of weeks, you'll need to start thinking about what to wear when running. This isn't an aesthetic thing – I never look like a sleek Nike ad when I run. I just don't care (although a jazzy print is appealing).

It's because running is a sweaty, chafing, foot-pressuring sport and also because you really don't want leggings that fall down or seams that rub until you get blisters. It matters because these things can slow you down, ruin a run and make it less fun. I spent years in shit leggings which I was hoiking up at every turn, not realising that I COULD DO BETTER.

First things first. Shoes. Shoes are so important. If you decide that running is your jam, your old gym shoes won't cut it for long. At best, they will be uncomfortable, at worst you'll get an injury. Now running trainers can be expensive – it's the one part of my hobby I shell out for regularly (most experts say that you need to replace your shoes after 300–500 miles).[2] The best thing you can do for your feet is to go to a specialist running shop and get them to analyse your gait (they put you on a treadmill and record your running style). This way, they can look at whether you roll your ankles or have flat feet, or whether you are a hobbit (no trainers can help you if so). Get all the info you need from the gait test and try on as many shoes as you can bear to – sometimes you just don't know until you've walked around the shop which ones 'feel' right for you. Please don't feel obliged to buy the shoes they recommend on the spot – if you search online you might just find them cheaper. *Runner's World* has lots of good advice on trainers, and if you look on Instagram, Emma Kirk Odunubi is a brilliant runner who does regular shoe reviews and Q&As to help you find the right pair.

After wearing out all the shoes I've run in over the past five years, I'm going to give you one personal note on trainers. I fell into the trap early on of buying running shoes I thought were pretty. Don't do that. Don't be stupid like me. This got me wearing shoes that weren't really right for me, and I've suffered from knee pain and shin splints (partly because of this). A few years ago, I stumbled upon HOKA trainers, and I will never buy another shoe again. That's dramatic, I might. I change my mind about stuff a ridiculous amount. But they are the bounciest, most comfortable trainer I have ever worn to run in. They look like huge marshmallows, and I wouldn't have picked them on style grounds, but I love them with a fire that burns. This is not sponcon (I WISH THEY WOULD SPONCON ME), it's just a little recommendation. They may not be for you, but I wish I'd known about them years ago.

Right, on to apparel. Less vital than footwear, but here are a few things that I find pretty important for a good run.

I'll try to be gender neutral here but we'll start with sports bras to get it out of the way. Don't fuck about with your boobs. I see women running sometimes without the proper support and I almost FEEL their pain. Even an 'OK' bra can be painful. You do not want your boobs to move much, if at all. According to Runners Need (a specialist running shop): 'The unique motion of running causes your breasts to move in a figure of eight motion, sometimes up and down as much eight inches.'[3] EIGHT INCHES.

Research at Portsmouth University has shown that women change the way they move depending on what support they have.[4] (I can attest to this, running hunched over to stop boob pain on a day I wore a normal bra.) So it's vital to have the right one. There are so many out there to choose from that it can get overwhelming. My advice is manifold:

- Don't even consider anything that isn't clearly labelled 'high impact'. Everything else is for slightly less energetic exercise – yes, that thin strappy bra looks nice but it's for YOGA, not bouncing down a hill.

- There are compression bras (which squish your boobs down) and encapsulation bras (which have two moulds for your boobs but with more support than a normal bra). Both are fine, but I find compression bras tend to take more of the bounce away.

- Make sure the bra is SNUG. It'll be a pain in the arse to get on over your head (you can buy ones that zip up the middle, which are great) but it'll be a blessing when you get going.

- Jump up and down when trying it on, even if you look bananas in the shop. It's worth it.

- From the feedback I got from bigger-chested women, Freya makes very good sports bras which support and have straps which don't cut into your shoulders. My favourite discovery of the past few years has been Maaree bras, which are like a second skin. I cannot feel anything when I run in these suckers, no jiggling, nada. And the creator is a one-woman band, who works phenomenally hard and seems lovely so it's even nicer to buy a bra off her.

- Get fitted if in doubt. Many places will fit your running bra for you – keep a note of your measurement so you can order more easily next time.

OK, bras done! The rest of my advice is less boob-focused so if you wandered off because the above didn't apply to you . . . come back!

WHEN IT'S COLD

It's easy to look outside (especially in the UK) and think that it's too cold and grim and you'll need a big jumper, but honestly you heat up fast when you're running. The amount of times I've been lumbered with jumpers and jackets wrapped around my waist as I run . . . it's annoying and cumbersome. Less is more, but if it's bitter outside, wear thin layers. Running snoods can be a lifesaver in winter, pulled up over your face. Windbreaker-style running jackets are usually enough to protect you from the elements. Don't plump for a thin fashiony one, go for something old school and with 'geography teacher in the 80s' vibes. Mine is from Karrimor and has never leaked, unlike some other big sporty brand ones which I won't name cos I don't want to be sued.

WHEN IT'S HOT

When it's hot – obvious time – wear very little. This again can feel exposing and scary but remember that . . .

NOBODY IS LOOKING AT YOU

So I'm talking shorts and a vest top and nothing else. It genuinely feels delightful running in next to nothing. The air on your skin is exhilarating – I swear I run faster in the warm breeze. Two things here:

- Wear SPF 50. The amount of terrible criss-cross tan marks I've been saddled with from forgetting is embarrassing and irresponsible. You won't notice you're burning, until you get home and then . . . OW. Consider a baseball cap for the same reason, and also cos you'll look like a hot 90s music video extra.

- Be prepared for chafing. It can strike at any time of year depending on the gear you're wearing, but obviously summer is a key danger zone. When you sweat, the areas of your body prone to rubbing are even more susceptible and the result can be fucking painful and enough to put you off running for a while. Chafing is most common around the inner thigh and crotch, armpits, under boobs, but you can experience it wherever flesh rubs together. The two most common approaches to this horrible rubbing are to make sure the skin is dry before a run – you can use a dry powder specifically designed for chafing (not talcum powder) – and to use lubricant on the affected areas. Many people recommend Bodyglide which you can find in sports shops and online. Avoid cotton clothes because they stay wet – clothes with wicking are your friends. Longer tight shorts help avoid rubbing, and for those unlucky enough to experience rubbed nipples, you can get covers. Not sexy by any means, but they do the job.

SOCKS

Who knew that socks were important? Not me, not for four years of running. I wore whatever came in a bundle by the tills. I lived in ignorance until a sports brand sent me about 50 pairs after I mentioned in an interview that I didn't see the point in them. But fuck, they were ridiculously effective. Not only did they keep my feet dry (honestly, runners have gross feet, it's just something you have to deal with and keep at bay with pedicures if you can be arsed), but they cushioned my feet from the blisters that sometimes crop up on runs (especially when you start out). You can get compression ones (which help with recovery), ones with silver in them for those prone to stinky feet, padded ones for the dreaded blisters, even ones to help

Socks...
but make it
FASHION

stabilise your feet. Magic! Of course, starting out you definitely don't need to worry about socks too much, but later on if you think any of these issues are affecting you, browse the wild array of choice. Capitalism!

LEGGINGS

Some people don't think they're acceptable everyday wear. Those people are wrong. Sorry, I just needed to say that. Good running leggings make a massive difference. You can get any pair, from anywhere – you do not need to spend a ton of money. But make sure that they are tight. You might feel like a sausage encased in skin but trust me, baggy leggings are the worst. Make sure they come up high. No hipster leggings here please. Squat down when you try them on to see how low they go. I think you shouldn't be able to see your belly button when standing. If you can, there's a good chance they'll slip down even further when you move. Get ones with side pockets and zip pockets on the back. The amount of shit you accrue on runs means you'll need places to put it all. Feel free to add a jazzy bumbag, but make sure it's a non-jiggly one – like the Flip Belt (£20), much loved by runners because it sits snugly on your waist and doesn't move. This all applies to men too – my husband looks banging in running leggings.

HEADPHONES

I honestly think that which headphones to buy are in the top five questions I get asked about running kit. I know very few people who run without headphones – amazing if you can, but it's not for everyone. I use wireless ones – i.e. no wires (I guess that much was obvious, huh). These can get expensive, but I always recommend the brand KitSound Metro (I promise I'm not being paid for any of these recommendations) because they're normally under £30 and last for hours. They don't slip off your head either, which is a danger when sweat is involved.

A TRACKER APP, WATCH, HOMING PIGEON . . .

Some people like to run without timing themselves or looking at how long they did. I think that's great – an aimless run with no target is a lovely thing, and good for the mind. We can all get obsessed with hitting a goal time, or going faster than last week, and while it's good to want to improve, lots of people fall into a trap of trying to beat themselves. And that is a sure-fire way to end up not enjoying the time you spend jogging. With that note of caution ringing in your ears, you'll probably want to have a look at how you're doing and there are lots of ways to do that. The easiest – and cheapest – is an app, and there are many available. I use Runkeeper – it's accurate and, most importantly, free. It's nice to see how many runs I've done, and it's interesting to see the days that were good and days that were bad and figure out why. Many runners use Strava, which shows you other people's routes and makes it feel a little more communal. And then there are fitness watches, but I think they're best left for down the line if you keep running and don't want to be bogged down by your phone. No need to invest in expensive tech just yet.

I could go on about tank tops, skorts (shorts under a skirt – so brilliantly 90s), T-shirts and running armbands, but I won't, because these things aren't as important and you can have fun choosing what you like the most as you go. Just remember, running is best when you can't really feel what you're wearing. Nothing on your body should be distracting you. Nothing should dig or pinch or rub or, worse, FALL DOWN. Comfort is key, but beyond that, the enticing world of neon and pattern and ridiculously upbeat motivational quote T-shirts is all up to you. Enjoy (or ignore).

PART SIX

LET'S GO RUNNING

So confidence – tick. Fear of being laughed at – gone. Kit – you have clothes on. The joy of running is that there's nothing else to prep. Maybe that's the scary part too – nothing more to string out before you've just got to start. So . . . now it's time to run.

I started with a three-minute run and then went home. I increased my runs over a few weeks and then realised I needed some more structure to my post-break-up experiment. For this, I downloaded the Couch to 5k app. There are a few variations of this app – they're free and you can download them on your phone.[5] In a nutshell, it's a programme which guides you through training and ends with you being able to run five kilometres in one go. It normally takes around nine weeks and gets you out there three times a week. If you want to run, and you want to keep running, this is a brilliant tool to start out with.

The first few sessions are mainly walking, so if you're feeling really intimidated by the idea of running for ages, don't be! The programme is slow and gentle and you can repeat weeks if it's going too fast for you. You can also skip weeks if you're a massive overachiever, though I don't recommend it. You know that saying: 'Don't run before you can walk'? That's true of running too – maybe 'Don't sprint before you can run.' It's good to take it slow. It's good to build it up.

I'd really advise you to give it a try – so many people get in touch with me to say that they're disappointed that they can't run for more than ten minutes, or feel like it's really hard to not lose their breath when they begin, and this app really helps you with all of that. Running is hard! Your body probably isn't used to this kind of exertion, and yet people expect so much from themselves. You wouldn't assume you could learn a language in two weeks, or become a brilliant painter overnight, so why would you berate yourself for not being able to run effortlessly on the first go?

In fact, go on. Write down five things you can't do and would expect to be able to do within a week. I'll start. I cannot knit. I do not think I could knit well within a week. I would not berate myself as a beginner. I cannot ice skate, and I'd be OK with a bad first attempt.

5 things I cannot do

①

②

③

④

⑤

Obviously if you're a little more spontaneous, or just don't like the idea of a person giving you orders in your ear as you go, then that's fine too. But if you don't want to follow the programme, then just make sure you try and remember three things:

- Go slow – if you overdo it initially, you're at risk of injury or, almost as bad, losing any enjoyment from it.

- Listen to your body and take rest days. Don't use up all your enthusiasm in the first few runs.

- Don't go too far – it might feel like you want to run forever, but hold back and meter it out over several weeks.

If you do choose to do the programme, remember that it's a guide, not a mandatory exercise. Running should never make you feel guilty – it should challenge you, yes. It'll be hard for sure. Sometimes you'll hate every minute. But above all, it should be your choice and you shouldn't ever do it because you feel like you're letting an app down. If you have to skip a week, that's fine. If you feel knackered from work one night, go tomorrow. If the pace of the programme is too fast, repeat as many runs as you need. If you need to go off programme for a few days and do a random loop around the block, that's great!

So, now it's time to do your first run. Or your first run with a new mentality. Whichever it is, remember to:

Start off with five minutes of walking to properly warm up. And then slowly start to jog. There's no race to be won, so go very slowly. This will mean you're less likely to lose your breath, get a stitch or just fucking hate it. Congratulate yourself as you go – one minute of running is a triumph when you've not done it for years – or in some cases, ever. OK – got your house keys? Blown out that candle? GO! This journal will be here when you get back.

PART SEVEN

YOU DID IT!

The first run is the hardest one. Because it's a statement that you're changing something, putting faith in something, hoping for something – all while you don't know if you can, or if it'll help. And yet you still went and ran. And if you've been scared and anxious for a long time, that IS something. However it felt, you did something good for yourself today. Go on, write down a tiny note of congratulations on the next page.

This is a box for you to draw some self - congratulations

And now shut this book down and eat some cheese, or drink a glass of wine. Pick it up again tomorrow.

(And by the way, if you ache tomorrow, that's totally fine and normal and just a-OK – no worrying about weird leg pain.)

PART EIGHT

PANIC VS. PUFF

Write down how your running is going here – give yourself one compliment and one target for the next run:

As we talked about before you went for a run, the physical effects of running can be a bit daunting. Now you've gone out and actually jogged, you might have experienced this yourself. So let's look at it a bit more. When you've never really run before (or done any kind of physical exertion beyond panic), you can feel very odd at first. The work your body has to do is heavy going – think about it, every bit of you is moving, trying to sync up, trying to keep upright and streamlined and desperately doing its best not to fall over. It's a lot. I remember the first time I ran I was amazed at how heavy my legs felt, and slightly alarmed at how hot I felt throughout my short initial attempt.

So as I mentioned earlier, it might be helpful here to just touch on some of the physical sensations that running can throw up – because often, and unhelpfully, they can feel very similar to those that anxiety can produce. It's good to know this early on, because if you feel out of breath or a bit like you're going bright red, you might start to think you're panicking when, in fact, your body is doing all the right things. Even if you didn't feel any of this on your first run, it's helpful to guard against any future worries. Probably you'll be unbothered by any thoughts like this, but I get messages about it a lot, and it definitely bothered me when I started, so let's just look at anxiety vs. exertion and think about how to differentiate between the two.

Firstly, take note of your breathing – for those of you who suffer from panic attacks, it might feel a little bit similar at first, which can be unnerving. Breathing is often the first thing an anxious person will check on. But a panic attack is an overreaction to fear, whereas your body is doing exactly what it's supposed to be doing when you're exercising. Think of it as almost as the flipside of a panic attack. Everything is working as it should – this isn't anxiety welling up, it's your body learning how to move, building up a sweat, powering you on.

I get lots of messages about how physical exertion can feel like panic, so let's just work through a few of these signals and look at the differences:

- Shortness of breath. When you're anxious, this happens because your body is trying to get more oxygen to your muscles in case you have to flee. Your heart rate increases, in case you have to fight. When you're running, being breathless is normally just a sign of exertion. Your body is working harder than usual to meet the increased demands of running. It feels hard, but as you get more used to it, your breathing will get easier. If it feels too much, walk for a bit until you feel calmer, always reminding yourself that this isn't panic.

- Chest pain.[6] When someone is anxious, it's common to experience stabbing pain in the chest, which often leads to worry that it's something more serious. Running can also cause chest pain, normally because you're not used to the exercise or because you're experiencing cramp. Heartburn is also a likely culprit. I often suffer from this if I've eaten a lot before a run, or drunk too much coffee.

- Sweating. This is something many people experience when gripped by anxiety. It's obviously also incredibly common when you're exercising – as your body tries to cool down. Embrace the sweat – it's a sign that you're working hard and pushing yourself. It's a good thing – even if you're so salty by the end that random dogs will want to lick your legs.

- Going red, flushing on the chest, feeling very hot – I get this when I panic AND when I run. Lucky me, huh? But feeling hot is so natural when you're moving vigorously and going red from exercise is completely NORMAL (even if we go home looking like beetroot).

If you are afflicted with the anxiety beast and feel any of these symptoms, remind yourself that, for once, this is not it. This is you being strong and active – reassure yourself that your body is behaving naturally. You might feel nervous about running, and that's totally fine, but this time, your anxiety is not the main thing going on here.

How was the run?	Did anything hurt?	Did anything make you anxious?

Aside from the physical stuff, some people get nervous about straying too far from home when they start running. I remember this feeling – it's a big reason why I ran up and down an alleyway near my house. Start off doing a loop of your neighbourhood. You can make that loop as small as you like – the easier you make these first few attempts, the more likely you are to carry on. Gradually, start to try and run a little bit further away from your imagined 'safety zone' – I'm just talking one street further, not too much more. Running is a really good way to push your comfort zone – your feet are in control and you're not focusing as much on perceived dangers when you're trying to stay upright and avoid potholes, commuters and road signs.

After your first couple of runs, write down how you felt both mentally and physically in the box on page 147. Now is a really good time to look back and note anything that was uncomfortable (you can't just write down 'running'), address any worries you had and try and resolve any physical twinges. That might be as simple as stretching properly before you go next time (YouTube has lots of good videos on pre-running stretches to try) or trying breathing exercises to calm you down every morning before a run if you're feeling overly anxious. Keeping a record of your first few runs will really help you to understand the things that you're finding challenging and motivate you to remedy them.

Have a think about how you could help those pains or worries next time:

Any changes you can make?

PART NINE

GETTING TO KNOW YOUR BODY

Write down how your running is going here – give yourself one compliment and one target for the next run:

I'm going to suggest an even more practical record to keep, too. It can take time to figure out what your body needs before a run – I really find that running on an empty stomach gives me a better experience, but other people can't run without a decent meal or without having drunk a lot of water. Likewise, some people find that hot weather can zap their energy or that being on their period makes exertion almost impossible (me, hi!). It's good to note this stuff – so that when (and it is a when, not an if) you have a dispiriting run you can make the connection between what was going on that day and the experience. Try running after breakfast, and another time when you've not yet eaten. See how you feel. See if your body needs extra protein before a run or whether you run better if you carry water with you. (If you do, the best bottle for my money is the wrist bottle – you can grip it properly and it won't slow you down.)

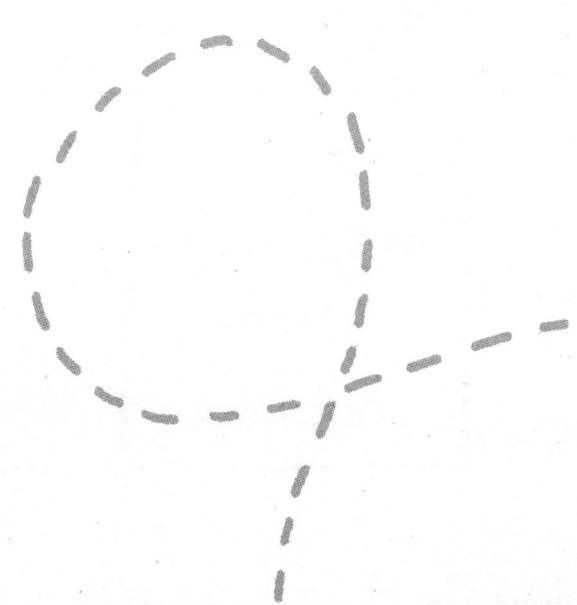

NOTE DOWN	RUN 1	RUN 2	RUN 3
what did you eat before?			
Did you drink enough?			
How was the weather?			
Anything else?			

PART TEN

HABIT

Write down how your running is going here – give yourself one compliment and one target for the next run:

In *Jog On*, I talked about how some research suggests that it takes an average of sixty-six days to form a new habit.[7] So if you're feeling confused as to why you're not taking to running like a duck to water on day six, don't be. Not loving it straight away doesn't mean you won't love it in time, nor does it mean that you're doing it wrong. Forming a running habit requires consistency and time. You're at the beginning of that journey, so instead of impatiently rushing to get there and being disappointed if you don't feel like you're nailing it yet, take a minute to feel proud of yourself.

It doesn't come naturally to me by the way, if you're rolling your eyes and feeling like self-praise is for Californians and nobody else. I cringe at patting myself on the back, but I've eased into doing it sparingly when it's really appropriate. And one of those times is running. I congratulated myself on five minutes running. Five kilometres made me feel like I could FLY. Running for over an hour still makes me feel like I'm a powerhouse. It's a feedback loop – I feel good from the run, I feel good and big myself up. I want to run again. That's a positive cycle – I'm not used to them. You've taken your first run. Maybe you've done a few. Take this opportunity to recognise what a big deal that is. Even if your idea of a nice compliment is just 'Well done on the not collapsing.'

Congratulate yourself here

AND WELL DONE FROM ME TOO. You've started some-thing, and that's not nothing. I'm thrilled that you're giving running a go.

PART ELEVEN

NOW WHAT?

Write down how your running is going here – give yourself one compliment and one target for the next run:

So you've taken your first run or two – which is already a massive feat. Seriously – just think about all the people in the world who haven't run since childhood. Now narrow it down. Think of all the people YOU know who haven't run since childhood. I bet it's half your social circle. And more than likely your dad (hi Dad). So even that first run is brilliant. But now you've got to keep going. I mean, you don't HAVE to – this isn't mandatory. But you're going to, right? So we've got to work at making this new habit stick.

Charles Duhigg, author of the bestselling book *The Power of Habit*, says: 'First, there is a cue, a trigger that tells your brain to go into automatic mode and which habit to use. Then there is the routine, which can be physical or mental or emotional. Finally, there is a reward, which helps your brain figure out if this particular loop is worth remembering for the future: THE HABIT LOOP.'[8]

There are a few things I would suggest you try in order to incorporate running into your life and help you keep it up long term.

• Try running at the same time every day. Learnt from journalling that morning jogs feel good? Great – try and pencil in your running for before work, or even incorporate it into your commute. If you make it a part of your routine, you might find it easier to get it done, instead of procrastinating (like I do sometimes when I could be running).

- Put your kit out the night before. It's a small thing, I know, but laying out my shoes and my leggings makes it easier to roll out of bed and head out. It's not dissimilar from going to sleep in your school uniform. Just me?

- Give yourself a reward after a run. It doesn't have to be massive – mine is normally an ice cream. But like a puppy at training class, we work better with treats. I'm sorry to inform you that we are no better than puppies. It's OK, we get ice cream and chocolate and they don't.

- Consider a running buddy to hold you accountable. There's lots of evidence that with a running buddy, you're more likely to commit to your workouts, keep up motivation and be consistent.[9] You might also enjoy it more with a friend who is also starting out. Some of my best runs have been with other people (though I primarily love running alone).

- Find a mantra. This can help you get out of the house and get running. It can also help you when you're ten minutes in and want to go home. I have two, and they repeat in my head when I'm not in the mood. My first is 'You never regret a run' which IS TRUE. And the second one is 'Just one more minute' – because sometimes when you're struggling, just one more minute can change the run and it's worth finding out if it's going to get better.

- Get stretching – before and after every run. I learnt from experience that this is really important. Don't be like me and think you don't need to. Sore knees will make you wish you'd prepped better.

In fact, come up with a mantra now. If it doesn't motivate you on your next run, you can change it later:

ONE MANTRA

Hopefully these things will help you keep going through those hard initial runs. And they ARE hard. Running is no easy thing. It hurts, you feel like you're wading through treacle sometimes, and a lot of the time you just want to stop! But as your annoying relative says at every family gathering, nothing worthwhile was ever easy. Oh look, now I'm your annoying relative. But it's worth it – otherwise I'd have given up on week two and would never have written this journal and instead I'd be eating crisps on the sofa (mmm, crisps).

So your next few runs will be fact-finding ones: finding your routine, figuring out what works for you. Remember to keep these runs short – whether you're following a set programme or not. And reward yourself, even if that means just two minutes at the end of the run sitting on a bench with your face towards the sun.

You might be finding it really hard in the beginning (totally normal!) – in which case, consider some of these steps:

- Repeat a one-minute run/two-minute walk strategy for six minutes and then go home, regardless of whether you feel you could do more.

- Cut your speed in half. THIS IS SO IMPORTANT. It might feel like you're basically speed-walking but shrug that off – it'll help build up your fitness and give you your breath back.

- Remember that most people find the first ten(ish) minutes of a run pretty difficult, so it's not surprising that you're struggling when you haven't been able to hit your stride yet.

- Consider doing some other exercise to improve your fitness levels – swimming, walking and biking can all really help your runs.

- If you're on a treadmill, think about getting outside. Many people find that running indoors can feel monotonous and relentless as opposed to outside, where the scenery is changing and the light helps your mood.

- Take your rest days – they're vital for muscle repair and to give your body a chance to recover.

- If you can, run in a place you find beautiful or visually interesting or GREEN. Nature is a powerful mood booster and jogging through a park or along a river can lift a run from ordinary to special. I sometimes run around the old City of London walls to see the incredible old buildings as I go.

It's also very helpful to assess your form after you've run a few times. People can quickly get obsessed with pace and endurance, sometimes to the detriment of good technique. Much is made of the correct way to run, and while I'm sure that it would help me to pay attention to the various research and ideas more closely, I never have (to my shame). But good technique isn't complicated, and doesn't require too much homework. It can make running feel less like a slog, and, even more importantly, guard you against some of the dreaded injuries that exercise can throw up (we'll talk about them later, don't worry).

- Look ahead – it's tempting to look down and see where your feet are going (especially on wobbly pavements) but looking down creates a strain and also makes it more likely you'll collide with someone or something (I have run into too many lampposts to mention).

- Try not to lean back or hunch forward – you might feel as though it's helping propel you, but it can cause lower back pain.

- Keep your hands relaxed and your arms by your sides at a 90-degree angle. Move them up and down, not across your body – this can make you out of breath.

- Try to strike the ground mid-foot – landing on the balls of your feet can cause shin pain and landing on the heel isn't ergodynamic.

- Shorten your stride – you might find you land better if you don't try and take such large steps. You don't want to be landing with a thud, more of a gentle tap.

- Relax your shoulders – we tend to start hunching as we go, but again, this can make your upper back tense up.

- Be gentle with your feet when you leap on and off pavements – the impact of road running is a little more intense than on grass and sudden pressure can hurt the knees.

This might all sound a little 'Goldilocks and the three bears' – not too hot, NOT TOO COLD – but these are just tips on how to get the best out of your runs. I don't advise spending your whole run concentrating on whether your arms are flailing or checking your stride obsessively (that would certainly detract from finding the joy), but it's worth keeping them in mind if you notice a twinge in your shoulders, or find your arms straying across your body wildly. Basically, you want to feel comfortable, not use up too much energy unnecessarily, and help lessen the chances of injury. A quick form check at a running shop (as mentioned in the 'Kit' section) can help you better understand what your feet are doing and whether you need to pay more attention to your gait.

- Relaxed body

- Mid Foot strike

- Short stride

PART TWELVE

THE DIFFICULT SECOND WEEK

Write down how your running is going here – give yourself one compliment and one target for the next run:

Right, you've done a few runs – you've felt out of breath, a bit self-conscious, but reminded yourself that . . . NOBODY IS LOOKING AT YOU. You've realised how much your body can sweat in mere minutes and you've felt pretty proud of yourself. This is all new and strange – a lifetime of thinking you're not a runner and now here you are, a person who has run. You're in a weird in-between zone where you've not mastered a new hobby but you're playing with it, exploring it, regretting it, then pencilling in your next attempt.

A few things about the first few weeks of running:

- It'll feel impossibly hard sometimes.
- You will feel impossibly proud sometimes.
- You will want to rush ahead but you must not.
- Parts of you will hurt.
- You will improve so fast.

This last point is the most important really. No matter how bad it feels on run two, on run three, you'll go for longer, or faster, or enjoy it more. No matter what yardstick you use to measure the success of your jogs, you will notice improvement. Concentrate on that. Write down those signs that you're getting better at it (remember, better doesn't have to mean faster).

Have you noticed signs of Improvement?

The other thing to note right about now is any pain you're feeling beyond the usual aches and blisters that new runners pick up. I'm not trying to scare you here – I literally wrote a book about lessening anxiety, it's not my motivation, I PROMISE – but it's common when starting out to find yourself with some injuries and this journal is not all unicorns and glitter (actually it's neither of these things at all). Good shoes, going slow, rest days and nice technique all guard against these, but it's inevitable that some of you will be unlucky and find yourself with a painful ankle, a grumbling knee or shin splints. I got struck down with the dreaded shin splints in the early weeks of running and I was FUMING to be laid up.

The most common running injuries are:

- A painful Achilles – the signs include a sore heel, sharp pain and swelling.

- Shin splints – so normal in beginners. A dull ache or throbbing pain, which gets worse if you try to run through it.

- Plantar fasciitis – heel pain, which worsens when you put weight on it. Swelling is also common.

- Strained muscles – most usually in the legs, and which can really hurt but heal pretty quickly if rested.

- Runner's knee – I'm afflicted – everyone dreads it. Can feel like a stabbing pain underneath the kneecap, or a dull pain all around it. Makes running impossible.

- Blisters – a common annoyance but can be bad enough to stop you running for a few days.

- Chafing – our bodies rub when we run, and chafing can be fucking painful.

- Stitches – yes they feel horrible, but they pass. Pull your body straight and take deep breaths. Stop for a minute if you need to.

Injuries are bloody awful, especially when you're starting out and feel like you're just beginning to get somewhere with running. But it's also a very obvious time to pick one up, when you're doing an exercise your body is not familiar with and you're working out your technique. Lots of people feel so put out by injuries that they do one of two things:

• Run through the problem.

• Give up running altogether.

Neither is a good resolution! Ignoring the injury and pushing on only serves to make the problem worse, until you're in too much pain to continue, or you need medical intervention. Giving up is a crying shame after all the hard work. Injuries happen – with any exercise – and often without it! I've hurt myself in many stupid ways that had nothing to do with physical exertion – I burst my own eardrum with a cotton bud – and getting a sore knee or a blister isn't a sign that you weren't meant to run. Don't give the setback too much importance. Instead, treat it properly and try not to let it get you down.

The good news is that most running injuries can be treated with rest, stretches, properly fitting shoes and good form.

• If you get pain somewhere, don't ignore it! Take a few days off and see how it's feeling before you go again.

• Don't try to increase your runs in length by anything more than a few minutes at a time – overdoing it can lead to problems.

- Invest in a foam roller and knead those tight muscles (or use a tennis ball – YouTube will show you how).

- Make sure your trainers fit properly – protect your feet, they do the hard bit.

- Hot baths with Epsom salts can help reduce pain a little.

- Stretch, stretch, stretch – pre and post run. Tight muscles exacerbate injury.

Three good stretches for running:

- Grab your left foot with your left hand

- Pull it towards your bum

- Hold it there and gently pull inwards

- Keep the position for 30 seconds

* Repeat on other side

②

- Stand on a step on the front of the foot

- Lower your heels

- Alternate each foot for 30 seconds

③

- Push your hands against a wall

- Push one foot forward and stretch your other leg back

- Back straight

- Swap legs

You can help safeguard against injury by doing extra exercise like weight training and squats, etc., but that's a lot to take on so early in your running exploration. Down the line, think about whether you'd like to add in some other stuff to help boost your running. The nice thing is, once you've started using your body more, exploring other ways to do it gradually becomes pretty appealing. Your body is made to be used, and when you awaken that instinct, you start to wonder how else you could strengthen it, work it, make it faster and healthier. I have really learnt to love walking purely because I enjoyed running and realised how nice doing it, but slower, could be.

If an injury puts you out for more than a week, you might consider seeing a doctor or a physio. I occasionally see a brilliant osteopath who really helps speed up the healing of any knee niggles I pick up. It's an expense, but it gets me back to running, which is vital for my mental health so I guess it's a tax write-off? (It's not, don't write that down unless you're competing in the Olympics.) Please don't worry too much though – it's rubbish, yes, but it probably won't hinder you for long, and it's just a sign your body isn't used to running yet. After my initial introduction to shin splints early on, I didn't encounter injury for another four years – that's four years of anxiety-easing runs without a twinge. It's worth waiting it out and keeping the faith.

If you're running for your mental health, having to stop abruptly because of an injury can feel incredibly frustrating – especially if you've already noticed that it's helping with mood or worry. Many people find that having to take a few weeks off can really impact their mental health – and I've experienced that myself. But even a bad injury doesn't have to mean no exercise at all. I found that cycling really helped my knee pain, for example. Swimming can also assist recovery from injury – and yoga and Pilates will help you keep active as well as stretching you out. And in periods when I can't run, I employ the other tools that keep my mental health boosted – I bake more, I employ mindfulness techniques, I sit outside in the sunshine to soak up some vitamin D. I walk in nature. These things don't give me the instant boost that running does, but they help for sure. There's a reason why relying on only one crutch for mental health is inadvisable – a toolbox of things that help means you'll always have something else to reach for. What would you employ if you had to take some time off exercise?

What positive things would
you do if not running?

There are some common running stretches which can help guard against injury and pain. You'll find tons more on YouTube, specialist running sites and on the NHS website. There is some evidence that dynamic stretches (moving rather than static) can help before a run – so think squats, calf raises, side stretches, quad stretches and walking lunges.

- Stand with your feet just wider than hip width

- push your bum down and out

- keep your chest up and shoulders back

- 10 times

After a run, static stretches are helpful. These can include: hamstring stretch, a hip flexor stretch and an IT band stretch.

These can help you reduce the tight feeling that running gives.

- Stand feet hip width apart
- take a step forward and hit ground with heel first
- lower down until the thigh is parallel to the ground
- 10 times each leg

Right, let's move on from the doom and gloom of injuries, shall we?

PART THIRTEEN

DIFFERENT WAYS OF RUNNING

Write down how your running is going here – give yourself one compliment and one target for the next run:

By now, I imagine you've done a few weeks of running – you're getting more accustomed to it, maybe you're even looking forward to heading out for a jog sometimes. You're no longer a total beginner – which should give you a boost. After concentrating on just getting through the first few runs, you can now think about how you want your future excursions to be. After your first few goes, you'll probably have a bit of an idea about whether you like running in the morning or evening. You might find that you enjoy a run around the local park, or prefer road running. It's such a personal thing, and finding out your perfect run will make it easier to motivate you.

My favourite run is first thing in the morning. I drink a pint of water, stretch a bit, procrastinate for half an hour, and then head out. I run completely aimlessly – going in any direction that feels good, staying on the flat, and I usually try to find a quiet or picturesque place to go through – a canal is good, or the park. I like to run for long enough to listen to a podcast or two, and then I buy myself some crisps and get the bus back from the place I end up finishing in. That gives me time to cool down and read the news before I get home and start work.

Your perfect run probably won't be mine – not everyone likes sitting on a bus in sweaty gym gear. But maybe you'll like the idea of an aimless run. Here are some things to consider:

- Running outside. Some of you will have started running on a treadmill. There's nothing wrong with that, but lots of people find that running outside provides more visual stimulation, different running routes and fresh air. You might feel nervous about venturing out right now, but consider it when you feel more confident in your running.

- Parkrun – a brilliant initiative with over 1400 different locations worldwide every week.[10] It's free and caters to all levels of ability and provides such an upbeat and supportive atmosphere. If you need a bit of a boost, Parkrun just might be the thing for you.

- Running in nature – this can be a park, a wood, a beach or just a local towpath. Research on the benefits of spending time outside in nature has shown that even five minutes can help lift your mood.[11] Running somewhere peaceful and beautiful can make your experience so much better than a run-down main road.

- Running with purpose – by this I mean using your runs to get from place A to place B. I often use running to get me across London when it's busy and I can't face wasting time on a train. Try out a run to a museum, or on your daily commute (if you can shower when you get there), or even just to the shops. It can add an extra sense of purpose to your runs which makes it easier to get out of the house and go.

- Try hill running. I sound like a sadist right now because it's my WORST, but it builds endurance like nothing else, and the powerful feeling it gives you at the top is amazing. And then you get to run down the hill screeching, 'Wheeeeee!'

- Try leaving your phone at home and just doing what your body wants you to do. No checking your time or looking at your duration. Just doing what feels good that day.

- Run on different surfaces. Your legs get accustomed to the same ground – mix it up and see what feels good.
- Run on a treadmill if you can't face the weather, see if you like it more than I do.

Whatever you try, remember to keep a slow and steady pace, and don't overdo it. I know this is boring and repetitive advice, but I say it because I know it's true from experience. The most common thing I hear from new runners is that they found running intoxicating, brilliant, whooshy and so they ramped it up and then either hurt themselves or found it too hard and lost that enjoyment. You've got a lifetime to push yourself, run races, try sprinting. Use this early phase to find the joy in it instead.

PART FOURTEEN

WHAT TO LISTEN TO

Write down how your running is going here – give yourself one compliment and one target for the next run:

There is a heated debate the world over, and it is between people who listen to music while running vs. people who listen to podcasts and audiobooks vs. people who listen to NOTH-ING. The war will never end and you have to pick a side.

OK, I'm being slightly dramatic here but, in truth, people do tend to fall into one of those categories. I started off listening to very angry music because I was unhappy and furious with the world and it motivated me to keep on going. It's a great tactic, and raging rhythms still fire me up to this day. But I also found that this kind of background noise had me keeping time with the beat, and that was making me run too fast. AND YOU KNOW HOW I FEEL ABOUT THAT. In week four of running, I found that I couldn't do more than ten minutes and I kept hobbling home, defeated and disappointed in myself. I couldn't figure out why, until I realised that, according to my running app, I was doing a kilometre in five minutes and forty-five seconds. Which isn't Olympic speed or anything, but it was far too fast so early in my running foray. And it was leaving me out of breath and making me get hungry and tired. And it was because I was keeping up with the angry music! So stupid, yet so simple. So I cut it out for a few weeks, slowed right down and listened to audiobooks instead. (I hear *Jog On* is frightfully well narrated . . .) And my pace slowed, and I increased the length of my runs and I thoroughly enjoyed it all again.

That is not to say that a good running playlist can't elevate a jog – far from it. Sometimes I put on my favourite mix and run like the wind. It's just a note of caution in case you encounter the same issue.

Ten songs that keep me going on a hard run:

- Solange – 'Losing You'

- Robyn – 'Dancing on My Own'

- Salt-N-Pepa – 'None of Your Business'

- Ice Cube – 'You Can Do It'

- Liz Phair – 'Fuck and Run'

- Lizzo – 'Worship'

- Taylor Swift – 'Shake It Off'

- No Doubt – 'Just a Girl'

- Lorde – 'Green Light'

- Prince – 'I Wanna Be Your Lover'

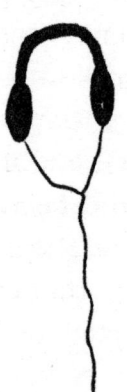

Many runners swear that music helps them – makes them work harder, elevates their mood and keeps the run fun. And research tends to back this up.[12] So there are solid reasons why you should compile a banging playlist and crank up the volume. But first you need to figure out if you want to run to the beat or not. If you do, you've got to figure out what your stride is. A simple way to calculate this is to count your steps while running at your normal pace for a minute. Then you'll want to sync this up with music which has roughly the same beats per minute – e.g. if you took 130 steps in a minute, you'll want music with the same BPM. There are tons of apps which will match you up with music, and Spotify offers this too. If this all just sounds a bit overwhelmingly technical and fiddly, then compile a list of songs that you love and that feel upbeat and pacey enough for a run – then ruthlessly prune and add to it. You figure out within seconds whether a song is right for your pace or whether it's hindering your session.

Podcasts are my jam. Can you tell I'm thirty-five? Nobody says JAM. But seriously, they keep me interested when running gets boring or hard. They don't make you rush on, but instead provide background distraction and they're free! I listen to a variety of politics and human interest ones. My favourites (perfectly timed for runs) include:

- The Daily – *New York Times* podcast on what's happening in the world.

- Slowburn – telling the story of Bill Clinton and Monica Lewinsky in a new light.

- You're Wrong About That – a podcast that explores stories we've all got some level of knowledge about but usually got the real details upside down.

- Keep It – a pop culture podcast that makes me laugh.

- Table Manners – a food and discussion show with the singer Jessie Ware and her fabulous mother cooking for their guests (disclaimer, I've been on it).

- Fresh Air – a long-running interview series with enough episodes to keep you going for years.

- Radio Atlantic – considered current affairs commentary from a magazine that's been around since 1857.

- My Favourite Murder – an irreverent and darkly comic podcast about famous murders.

The BBC also has its entire library available on the BBC Sounds app so you can listen to everything from sport to documentaries while you huff and puff up a hill. Check out 'Inside the ethics committee' for a selection of fascinating moral quandaries. If you'd rather listen to audiobooks, Audible has a massive library of titles, though iTunes is often cheaper for one-off purchases. I listen to thrillers when I run sometimes, they keep my heart rate up . . .

If you choose to run without any audio, then you're already better than the rest of us (I'm kidding, kinda). You probably want to connect with the run more intensely, or maybe you want to use the time to work through a problem or give your thoughts time to percolate. It can be freeing – you'll run to your own beat and not that of music or chat. You might notice your surroundings more as you go – there's nothing better than discovering little details about a place on a run that you might not have noticed before. It might feel more challenging to start out with (which is why I don't do it very often) but it's worth exploring – even just to decide that it's not for you. Whatever you decide works for you, just remember that safety is more important than any favourite track – you need to be able to hear traffic so make sure you stay aware. I run with over-ear headphones and leave one slightly off-centre so that I can always stay alert to noise around me.

- **Find** podcasts that grip you and carry you on

- keep music uptempo and encouraging

- Try silent running and see if it changes your experiences

PART FIFTEEN

ON THE WAY TO 5K

Write down how your running is going here – give yourself one compliment and one target for the next run:

Let's check in on your progress. With any luck (and with good trainers you don't need luck), you've not picked up an injury beyond a few blisters and stitches (terrible band name right there), and you're able to run for more than five minutes in a row. Don't worry if you're not doing that yet – you're not in a race, not even with yourself. There is no fixed end here, and if it takes you longer, then you'll have a solid foundation to build on.

How is running making you feel? I mean both physically and mentally. Do you find you have more energy? Are you sleeping better? Perhaps your legs hurt but you can feel your stamina increasing, and maybe climbing stairs feels easier. How is your mind doing? I'm going to go out on a limb and say that you already feel a bit lighter after a run – a bit less anxious during the day. If you have panic attacks, have you noticed a change in frequency? Do you think that you can differentiate panic symptoms and running sensations well now? Perhaps you feel like you're handling anxiety better, or noticing that a run gives your head time to work through an issue without heading straight into catastrophe territory. Maybe you're just feeling more confident in your ability to keep going, and noticing that seep into other areas of your life. Write down the changes you've noticed since you started running:

Any changes You've noticed

Now, is there anything you think isn't working for you? Often I hear from people halfway through a Couch to 5k programme, or from those who've been running for a few weeks off their own bat, and they think they're losing the motivation. I get that. You can't run races yet, it still feels hard, and maybe you still haven't had a whooshy run of joy yet.

Let's troubleshoot for a minute. Write down one or two (you can't have twenty, then you're just grumbling) things about running that you'd like to improve or change:

What do you want to change?

OK – how are you going to make that change? Because even if you wrote down 'I hate running and I have a powerful dread every time I go out' there's still a way to do something to make it better. Get bored halfway through a run? Stop for a minute, turn on the happiest song you've got on your device and sing along (out loud or in your head) before you set off again. Feeling sluggish? Drink a pint of water and shake your body for a minute. Finding it hard to get out of the house? Put your trainers by the door and run to the next street. See if you want to carry on road by road. Finding the rain too much? Lean into it – run through puddles and be fully soaked. There's always something you can do.

With that in mind, write down a few possible solutions to your niggles and try them out – see what helps.

How you might improve your running experience?

Here comes the stern pep talk . . .

Running is HARD WORK. It's no expert massaging your shoulders while kittens purr on your lap. It's not a doughnut and a cup of tea on the sofa wrapped in a blanket.

SomeTimes it Sucks

I told you I don't like sappy motivational quotes. But it's no bad thing to acknowledge that sometimes it's rubbish, or boring, or just not whooshy. Otherwise I suspect that for those people seeking an instant high, it just looks like something they're failing at. If everyone goes on about how miraculous a run can be and never tells you about all the bad bits, it can end up making people feel excluded. And there's nothing more demotivating than thinking that everyone has cracked the secret to something except you.

So I will happily admit that, sometimes, running is monotonous. And I almost never jump out of bed with the joys of spring ready to go. Often, I endure it rather than enjoy it. Grit my teeth and get through it. Running is not something you ever 'nail' – and that can be frustrating. It's hard to predict why a run is crap – though there are some usual suspects:

- A hangover will make a run harder, sweatier, slower.
- Your menstrual cycle (if you have one) will make you feel weaker, hungrier, less likely to be able to go as far as normal.
- Boiling hot days or freezing cold days will impact your enjoyment sometimes.
- Too little sleep can make exercise feel like a slog.
- Going for a run just because you feel like you SHOULD can make a run difficult.
- Being hungry or thirsty can fuck up a run.
- Needing to use the loo can be rubbish – I've gotten good at knowing where ALL the toilets are across London for just such a time.

The worst reason is that sometimes there's just no reason why a run turns out shit. That's what I mean when I say you can never 'nail' running. It's like trying to conquer Everest. But, like the mountain, it's not really there to be conquered. In fact, one of the most fascinating things about running is how unpredictable it is. I don't like change – most anxious people don't – but

I have learnt to accept that running can never be the same. I have a different experience with it every day that I do it. And that's a blessing in disguise – if I somehow felt that I'd cracked it, and felt the same level of emotion every time, then I think it would lose its power somewhat. One of the things that keeps me going is that it throws up new challenges, new feelings, new achievements and makes me find new tools to employ. Some days are shit, some days are brilliant. Just like everything else in life.

And for all the runs that feel terrible, there are runs that feel AMAZING. Where I feel whooshy and full of beans, then I'm invincible. Anxiety is banished for a bit, life feels full of hope and I feel free in a way I never could when boxed in by poor mental health. Those runs are the aim, the reason we keep going. But the other runs count just as much. The OK runs make you feel like you've accomplished something every time you put your trainers on. The hard runs make the ice cream/ hot bath/glass of wine even better. And the really crap runs force you to smile and shake off disappointment and try again another day. And the best part of it all is, you get the mental-health benefits from every single one of these runs. You still get the hormone boost. You still had ten or twenty or sixty minutes out of your busy day just for you. You still shook off some of that adrenaline that follows you around and you still fucking did it, even if you didn't want to.

Write down three things that make a run worthwhile (on a totally shallow level – I'm talking basic shit, like getting an iced coffee afterwards).

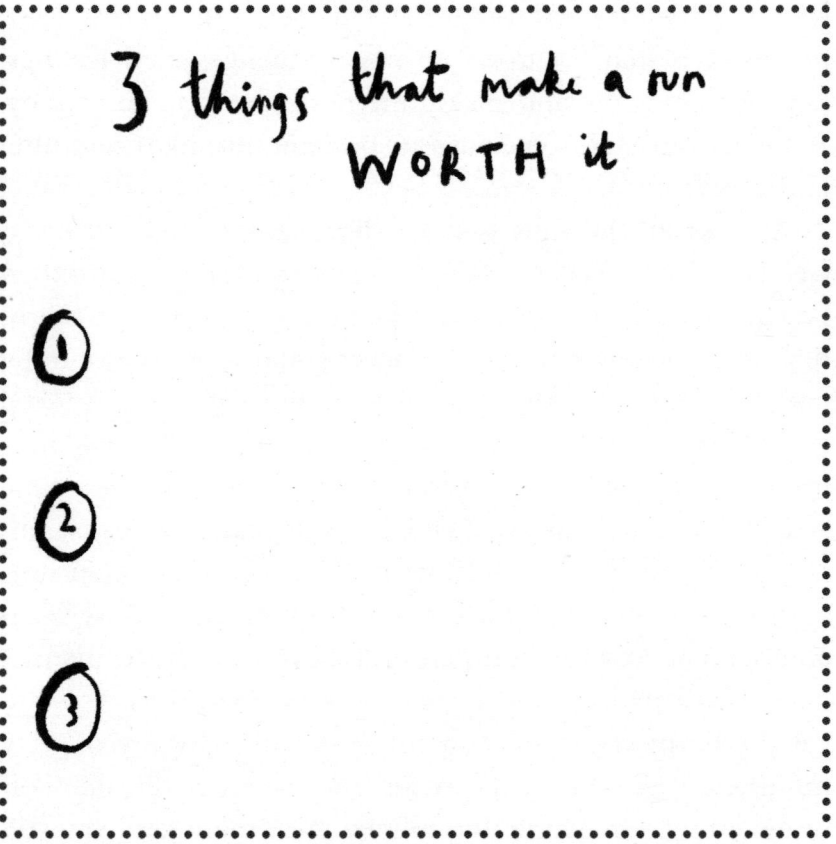

Now write down three things that make a run worthwhile on a deeper level (like getting time alone, or feeling more independent).

3 things that make running
WORTHWHILE

①

②

③

PART SIXTEEN

———

BOREDOM

Write down how your running is going here – give yourself one compliment and one target for the next run:

Sometimes, runs are BORING. Again, I'm telling you this to bust the myths that all runners are bopping around in a trance of happy delirium. Some runs, I am bored shitless. I plod on, look at my watch and see I've only done thirty seconds and despair at how slowly it's going. Now at this stage I can suggest the usual tricks to distract you – audiobooks, changing up your route, running to a destination. But I'm going to add in another angle. You can try and lean into the boredom. Just as I think it's important to acknowledge that running is hard, I think it can be helpful to embrace the boredom. Running is not a hobby that promised to always entertain you. You're thinking of Netflix – millions of hours of content served up to keep you amused.

Running is like anything else. Fun sometimes, hard often, MAGICALLY brilliant occasionally, boring a lot.

Oh, I like that. That's MY KIND OF MOTIVATIONAL QUOTE.

The boredom might be because the run is repetitive. It might be because you're so used to using your phone to entertain you every second you feel like you're unoccupied (me too). It's likely that you're not used to having so much time alone with your thoughts and it makes you feel uneasy – this can lead us to cast around for distraction. And that's often what boredom really is. An inability to be in the moment, just us. Acknowledge that, really think about how often you have time in the day to just be on your own with nothing to do but sit with your 'stuff'. I bet it's not often – us anxious people are very good at multi-tasking and keeping busy to put off thinking and feeling things that are difficult or serious. And running can really shake that up, forcing us to allow all of that stuff in. Sometimes that feels daunting.

But, like mindfulness, running can be a way to allow the thoughts in, and let them float away without engaging with them too much. It's hard to run and furiously argue with yourself. It's hard to run and keep upright and push on while worrying obsessively. All of your anxieties will still be there of course (running is not magic beans, as I wrote in *Jog On* many times), but they pop up, and then dissipate when you're moving. Why I don't know. Maybe because your body is in the driver's seat. Maybe because you haven't got the energy to engage them when you're using it all to power you up a hill. Maybe because the run is making you feel kind of kick-ass and strong and the scary thoughts you have normally can't affect you as they usually do.

So try and embrace a boring run. It might feel like it's going on forever, but it will end and you'll feel proud of getting through it. Use the time to listen to your breathing, or notice your form, or just get comfortable being with your thoughts. Notice how they pop up and then slide away. See how less bothered you are by them when you're moving. If that's all too uncomfortable, ask yourself a question, or think about a subject you're interested in and explore it as you go. Sometimes I even ruminate on a specific problem I have and find that I have the answer at the end of a run. Whatever you do, remember:

> *Being bored doesn't make you a bad runner. It doesn't mean you can't run or that you're not made to run. It just means that some runs are dull, just like everything else in life. And sometimes boredom can mask the very real reluctance we have about being unstimulated.*

Think about three topics you might be interested in thinking about on your next run. It doesn't matter if your mind veers off, but giving a run a theme can be a nice way of having a more interesting run while still engaging with your own thoughts.

3 themes for your thoughts
when running

①

②

③

And remember, today's run might be dull and then boom, tomorrow the wind whips around you, and the sun comes out, and you see a baby duckling wiggling after its mother on a canal and you run past an ancient building and everything feels ALIVE and exciting and like this exact moment is humming with possibilities and you wonder how you ever felt bored or like this was hard. If you have a bad run, or a hard run, or a dull run, write down a time (even if it was just a five-minute burst) where running felt brilliant. We tend to focus on the negative, and forget the times that we enjoyed something if the most recent example of it was less than excellent. Change that instinct – work to balance out your thoughts here.

Describe a good run you've had

PART SEVENTEEN

LONGER-TERM
MOTIVATION

Write down how your running is going here – give yourself
one compliment and one target for the next run:

Whether a run is dull or great, it's vital to remind yourself why you're doing all of this. Running can get hard and, when it does, look back at the reasons you wrote down in this journal for starting in the first place. Remember that the hardest bit is at the beginning, before you've seen the benefits that I bang on about, but remind yourself that you WILL see them. Give the habit time to form first.

At the risk of sounding like the leader of a dodgy pyramid scheme, it helps to see how hard it is and use that as fuel. You're doing something that most people don't want to attempt – and you're doing it to improve your mood and make your life a bit better. Those are big things, and worth the slog. Instead of thinking, 'Oh balls, it's raining and I just can't face the effort', try approaching the run in a different way. I'm not suggesting you run on a broken leg, or actively seek out painful or gruelling runs, but even a fifteen-minute jog can feel pretty tough, and I think we should take some pride in that. There's something very freeing in acknowledging that a run is difficult, that you're really having to push yourself to continue, that you'd rather be at home with the aforementioned crisps. Sometimes, instead of trying to be your own hypeman, it's good to say, 'Yup, this is fucking difficult and yet I am still going.'

Think about the difficult things you've done in your life that have been worthwhile in the longer term. Write a couple down. I'll start:

I trained a rescue dog over four months pretty intensively. The dog was a teenage idiot when we got him, and my life was taken over by this slobbering unit – it was fucking difficult to

tire him out, to get him to come back to
me in the park, to make him feel secure and
happy with us. And I cried a lot, and fought
with my husband about who would pick up
shit, and wondered why on earth we'd done
this to ourselves. But he's over the worst
of it now (I THINK), and he's lovely. Bouncy
and stupid and happy and he makes our house fun.
In the midst of pee and barking, I kept having to tell myself,
'This will be worth it when he's one. This will pay off for the
rest of his life with us.'

What have you done that was HARD but WORTH it?

People will have different reasons for running – from weight loss to cardio benefits – but if you're following along with this journal, your motivation is probably more closely connected to your mental health. I've said before that exercise is one of the main things that doctors recommend for improving your mental health, and I've also mentioned why that is – because it promotes better sleep, it gives you a boost of endorphins, it helps raise self-esteem, and it connects you with the world around you. But it's easy to hear those things and think, 'Yeah but I'm in a rut, things are too bad for me', or maybe even just to dismiss those results as too simplistic, too obvious, not big enough.

At my worst moments, if you'd told me that running (or cycling or trampolining) would've helped me, I'd have rolled my eyes and told you that you were being ridiculous. My head was full of weird and awful thoughts. I had panic attacks all the time. I was almost agoraphobic. The idea that moving and sweating could lift those things felt as stupid as suggesting that I cheer up. (Some people STILL say this to those struggling with mental-health issues and it KILLS ME.) So I can totally understand why people feel like there's no point in trying. But you're here, and you've already done at least one run, so let's explore the mental-health motivations a bit more.

Within a short time of running, you should begin to notice that your mood after a run lifts a little. Much is made of 'the runner's high' – a feeling of euphoria which lessens anxiety and reduces pain and basically is what we all chase.[13] Once you've felt it, you can be disappointed when you don't feel it every time, but you still get the mood benefits even on the days when you don't get that massive high. When you're feeling low, or especially anxious one morning, sometimes the idea of getting up and running can feel impossible – and I've experienced this so many times. People often ask me how to dig deep and find the energy to do it, and the best example I can give is a recent period in my life where I was very down and being bombarded by intrusive thoughts.

I went out every day running even though my mind was in turmoil, and I ran badly, with no joy, often with tears streaming down my face as if I was in a bad movie. And it didn't feel great – I have to be honest. But it was the only thing that gave me some time away from being enveloped by the thoughts and the sadness. I was running away basically – running away in order to come back again. And I didn't feel much better in the moment, but it kept me propped up. Enough that the dark period came and went faster than previous episodes. I kept going, and ran through it.

Think about some of your anxious or low moments. What have you done while you're in them? Do you tend to hunker down and shut the world out? Do you carry on as before, faking it until you make it somewhat? Do you try and utilise your coping skills to make the shit period a little bit more manageable, knowing that it will pass, with time and help?

What helps?

What doesn't?

```
. . . . . . . . . . . . . . . . . . . . . . . . . . . . . . . . . . . . . . . . .
.                                                                               .
.                                                                               .
.                                                                               .
.                                                                               .
.                                                                               .
.                                                                               .
.                                                                               .
.                                                                               .
.                                                                               .
.                                                                               .
.                                                                               .
.                                                                               .
.                                                                               .
. . . . . . . . . . . . . . . . . . . . . . . . . . . . . . . . . . . . . . . . .
```

I bet if you look at what you've written down above, the tools that help are things like: sleeping well, spending time with loved ones, talking, keeping a routine, returning to comforting films and books, doing things with your hands.

I bet that when you look at what doesn't help, some of you will have written down: avoidance, hoping it goes away, hiding at home, not telling anyone how you're feeling.

Happily, running falls into the first category, but, in order for it to help, it's not something you can only do on sunny days when you've got bundles of energy. It's a tool which works more and more effectively if you do it consistently. That doesn't mean you have to run every day, or even every other day. But it means committing to a regular schedule – I'd suggest three times a week at first. It means going out when you're feeling rubbish – like I described above. If you feel happy and skip a few months of running, it's harder to get back into it, and it won't be able to help you day to day with your anxieties and mood.

Running is not a vaccine – a long period of jogging won't make you less likely to experience episodes of poor mental health if you then stop altogether – but it *will* maintain your mood and help you cope with worry if you do it consistently. So that's my motivation. When I'm at a low point and don't want to go, and just want to crawl under the duvet and go to sleep, I remember that running is my mental-health maintenance. It's like a car service – if you never take your old banger to the garage, don't be surprised if something goes wrong with it one day.

Sometimes, when we're mentally unwell, we lean towards the very things that prolong and exacerbate the worries or unhappy thoughts we're having, and it's so, so hard to break out of that cycle. Keep reminding yourself that you have tools which can help, and commit to using them regularly.

Why don't you try three runs a week for a month and see what you notice. That's twelve runs – which hopefully feels manageable. As I've said, they don't have to be long runs – nobody is demanding you run for miles and miles. It's more important to be regular and to be able to fit it into the rest of your life. So fifteen minutes would be fine. Write down a brief summary each week – for this, you don't need to detail your form or bother about your pace. Just note how you felt at the end of each week, and whether it got easier to do within a schedule. After a month, think about how your mood has been, whether it has been easier to manage your mental health over the timeframe, and how you've been feeling in between runs.

So motivation doesn't have to come from weight loss, or races, or getting better or faster. Sure, those things can be part of it if they help, but try to run in a way that boosts your mental health. And that means being intuitive, doing it in a way that feels manageable, enjoying your runs and not comparing yourself to others. Sometimes that might mean going home and cutting a run short early if it's just not working for you – I don't advocate always pushing through discomfort. Again, listen to your body – if it's just dull, I'd push on. If you're incredibly low on energy and getting no enjoyment from it at all, you might want to walk for a bit. If it's just not your day, I think going home is fine. If you have a spell of these crappy runs (and many people do), then stop for a few days and rest – it's OK, it doesn't mean you're back to square one.

PART EIGHTEEN

WHAT COMES NEXT

Write down how your running is going here – give yourself one compliment and one target for the next run:

By now, I hope you've started to feel like you're a runner – you are, whether you've done two runs or twenty. Have you managed a kilometre without stopping? Or maybe your initial aim was to just be able to run to the end of the road despite any fears you've been storing up. Whatever you've achieved, YOU BETTER FEEL PROUD OF IT. I feel proud of every single person who starts running despite the fear that so many of us live with – it feels like you're putting faith in an unknown and also having faith in yourself. Oh God, I better stop now – I'm getting motivational quotey again.

So you're on your way to 5k – or maybe you've already got there. I don't know when we decided that five kilometres was the first goal of running. Maybe because it takes around thirty minutes and that seems like a decent chunk of time. But if you've got to three kilometres and feel great at that level, don't rush forward. Be happy with what you've already done before you hasten on towards the next hurdle.

I hope that running has given you confidence in your own abilities – you've done something scary, and you've pushed yourself hard and you're still going. I hope that helps you recognise what else you can do too. This might be to do with running, or it might be using that new confidence to test yourself in other ways.

I mentioned earlier in this journal that trying things that scare you is good for anxiety. It seems counterintuitive – we spend our whole lives trying to protect ourselves from danger – but, actually, confronting the things we're fearful about serves to show us that the worry has been built up in our mind. Running is a practical example of that – you've started something which felt daunting and you've managed it. So what else can you do?

If we're talking about running – have you found that you secretly really love getting faster despite my repeated bossy protestations that you must SLOW DOWN? Are you humming with excitement when you run further than before? Do you like beating your family at Jenga at Christmas and making your eight-year-old nephew cry? Then maybe . . . maybe you should think about a race.

Disclaimer – I don't do races. Never have, probably never will. It's just not my vibe. I run alone, and slowly, and I do it just for my head. And I worry that if I had to train for a big race I would lose the enjoyment I get from it. But that's just me, and I hope you've taken one thing from this journal, and that is that there's no right way to be a runner. If you think a race might be fun, or increase your motivation, or you just fancy the camaraderie of jogging with a bunch of other people, then go for it! And a race doesn't need to be a marathon – there are tonnes of 5k races to start off with and see if you like it.

If you're thinking about it, but you're still unsure, here are some of the reasons why people take part in them:

- It's a chance to test your limits. You want to see where running can take you? A race will help you down that path.

- It's a motivation like no other. You've got a fixed deadline and you've got to train for it.

- You'll make new friends – the race community is wide and welcoming and you'll meet so many new people through it.

- You'll take on new challenges. And hopefully hit them and progress to new and bigger ones.

- The crowd will cheer you on. Have you ever been to watch a race? The support from the spectators is genuinely amazing, and it gees you on.

- You see tangible results. My endless plodding never ends with a medal, or a better level of fitness. Hmm, maybe I'm talking MYSELF into a race now.

If a race isn't really your thing, then what about joining a running club local to you? That way you'll meet new people and have a schedule to stick to – and running with other people really does spur you on. They cater to all levels, so don't be worried that you're too much of a newbie, or that you'll be left behind.

Once I'd reached 5k with no stopping (just wait until you do – it's the best feeling) I decided to work up to 10k, mainly because it felt like a good wholesome number. It took longer than my initial goal – the advice is not to assume you can fast-track this training just because you've hit your stride. Try not to add more than a 10 per cent increase week on week – eight to ten weeks of building up to 10k is sensible and achievable. Stay slow – increasing the duration of your runs doesn't mean picking up speed (I actually got slower as I reached 10k) – and take rest days. It doesn't matter if it takes you longer to get to your next goal – the more practice, the better prepared you are long term.

If you want to challenge yourself and improve your fitness, you might consider interval training or fartlek training. In interval training, you run in high-intensity bursts for a short period and then allow your heart rate to return to normal before doing it all again. So you might run as fast as you can for thirty seconds, recover, and go again. Repeat this six times. Fartlek is similar, but less structured – you run as fast as you can without timing it, and then walk for a bit before speeding up. For this, you might want to run to a lamppost and then stop, walking to the next lamppost and so on. It can help to have a series of landmarks to guide you so you don't push yourself too far. If you REALLY want a challenge, another tactic is to run for short bursts, and then add in another exercise like star jumps or burpees. A killer, but you'll feel amazing afterwards (please only do this if your fitness levels are already pretty good). Interval training is credited with making your stamina and speed better, and it's great if you don't have the time for long runs – an interval run can be done in fifteen minutes and you'll still get all the mood-boosting benefits.

If you're happy running for your mind, and don't need a competitive challenge or new running buddies, that's totally fine – I don't actively seek out new and harder levels myself. If I end up going further than normal, I feel quietly pleased, and if I can do a run faster than previously, that feels nice too. But on the whole, my running hasn't progressed much since I started. Some runners would think that's a waste, but I run for me and nobody else. And you run only for yourself too. If 5k is where you land and you think, 'Perfect, that's what my running time will be', then that's FAB. But sometimes it's good to stretch yourself a little bit with any hobby – that doesn't have to be a race, it could just be a pledge to run for two minutes more than yesterday, or to run a new route every week. Or even a vow that you'll wear shorts when it's hot and enjoy the breeze without feeling self-conscious. Consider having three ideas in mind that will push you and add an extra element to your running:

3 ideas to challenge
you when you run

①

②

③

PART NINETEEN

SCARING YOURSELF
ON PURPOSE

Write down how your running is going here – give yourself one compliment and one target for the next run:

Right, now let's look at challenging yourself in other ways. When I started running, I was scared of EVERYTHING. And I knew that people said that exercise could help improve mental health but I didn't *reeaallly* believe it and I didn't think it would help ME specifically. And yet, as I've said, I felt the effects remarkably fast. My panic attacks slacked off, and I could shrug off intrusive thoughts faster and I felt OPTIMISM, which was rare as hell for me.

For me, every run I took felt like a mini miracle. It was a brave thing (on a very small scale) to push back against all my long-held fears and see if there was a way through them. I guess I was feeling the fear and doing it anyway (here I am, just leaning into the motivational quotes now). And as I've said, every bold step I took, I realised that I was meeting the challenge and doing well. And that made me test out my limits in other ways. So I would go to a crowded place and see how I felt (normally I'd panic) or I'd take a lift and not catastrophise about it jamming. And it wouldn't. And from those small steps, I took big ones – like flying alone, taking a new job where I didn't know anyone, flying on a MOTHERFUCKING TRAPEZE.

The point of this is to say: try and do some things that scare you. You've started running – a very hard, intimidating and strenuous challenge – despite your worries and fears. You can and will get to 5k as long as you keep going. Even if you never believed that to be possible. So what else can you do now?

I guess I was trying a form of exposure therapy. This sounds wacky, but it's basically a way to get you over phobias by retraining your brain so that it doesn't see danger where there is none.

Say you're scared of escalators (some people are!) – this practice would aim to get you on one by slowly desensitising you to the fear.

- You might start off by talking about escalators, or looking at photos.

- You could describe a journey on one.

- You could use CBT techniques to imagine a scenario which shows a rational result rather than your initial fearful one.

- You might stand near one.

- And eventually, you go on one for a short ride and then increase your use of them until they're boring.

This is what I did with the Tube, after sixteen years of avoiding it. I would run somewhere, and take the Tube for one stop when I finished. When that didn't feel scary, I'd take it for two stops. And now it's just a boring commute with sweaty strangers. Progress!

I know how strong running made me feel, and how it gave me the confidence to try other things. People tell you to exercise for all sorts of reasons but you don't often hear that it's not just about fitness and a mood boost – it's a foundation to build on. What else do you want to tackle? Are you someone who can't fly? Do you avoid crowded places or are too full of worry to drive alone? I've been all of those things. And I don't want to bounce you into trying things before you're ready to tackle them. I just want you to know that your commitment to running makes you stronger and more capable than you think, and that it will open up doors you never thought possible. And it's worth keeping that in mind and figuring out what you might like to do with that strength. Use it – and see what else you can do, what else isn't as scary as you thought, and learn what else can open up for you.

What might you confront next?

PART TWENTY

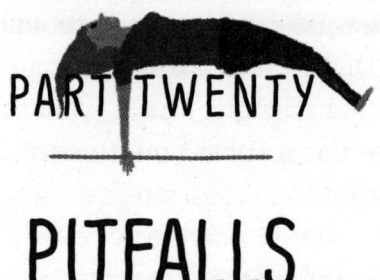

PITFALLS

Write down how your running is going here – give yourself one compliment and one target for the next run:

That sounds a bit negative for a journal encouraging you to run but I feel confident that you're well on your way now, and I want to note a few things that I've experienced and a few issues that readers of *Jog On* have raised too.

Running is the best thing I have ever done. It hooked me in, changed my life and enabled me to shake off paralysing fear. But there are some downsides to everything, and running is no different. So since, as previously mentioned, life is not rainbows and glitter, let's just talk about some stuff that running can throw up.

I get lots of messages from readers about being disappointed with how slow they are/how they can't run for as long as other people/how they don't look like other runners. I think we've adequately addressed that running is not a competition (you know, except when it actually is) and that the only person you have to please is yourself. I hope you keep telling yourself that.

For those who don't look like the slim (and often white) runners you might see on the covers of magazines, it can be frustrating. You are a runner no matter what society sees as the stereotype. You don't need to shrink or wear expensive athleisure brands. You don't need to explain your reasons for running to others, nor do you have to compare yourselves to anyone else. The great thing about running is that it's for everyone – and the bodies I see out running every day show me that. Change what you're looking at: check out the cross-section of society at a Parkrun, or follow body positive runners on Instagram – Latoya Shauntay Snell is an amazing runner who lifts me up every time I watch her videos. Please don't fall into the trap of using running to burn off calories – it takes away the pure joy of running and makes it a slog. I'm not saying that running can't make you fitter or sleeker, just that if it becomes the main goal, the mental-health benefits go out the window fast.

For those who feel like they're not good enough at running – remember that you're doing it, and that's already better than most people. You only need to be good enough to enjoy it – whatever that means for YOU.

To anyone who feels like running is not helping their mental health as much as it's helped mine – that's not a failure or a problem with the way you're doing it. Some people will get a bigger boost from it than others, just as yoga has never really helped me but has transformed life for many other people. Weigh up whether it's giving you enough joy and relief to be worth it – and if it's not, you can try other things. Life is long, and there are so many tools you can pick up and employ. Your running might be swimming, or boxing, or walking. It's not a mark against you if something else works better than jogging. And you gave it a good go – that's an achievement either way.

Now I'm going to be sneaky here and add something in that I didn't tell you about before. But I didn't want to scare you early on and now you're a pro so we can talk about it. Sometimes, NOT OFTEN, dickheads will honk vans at you or yell when you're running. Look, it's always men, OK? I'm sorry if you're a man and this makes you indignant, but it just is. It can be annoying, off-putting and sometimes scary. And enraging – don't forget enraging. And people get really victim blamey about it – as though we runners encourage it. Fuck that. It's happened to me, it might happen to you. If it does, ignore it – for your own safety and blood pressure. They WANT to shake you up, so don't let them. If you feel unsafe, that's one thing, but if it's just a dickhead with nothing better to do with his life, then let it pass you by. The great thing about running is that you're gone in seconds – off to the next kilometre, the next rush of joy, a place those losers will never reach. I'm not trying to minimise how shit it is, but it's rare and a book about men trying to freak women out would be a whole other thing, take YEARS and is not this one.

There can be other pitfalls – and I think the main one is getting obsessed with running. You may laugh at that at the moment, dreading the moment you've got to put your trainers on and start, but it sneaks up on you. And I've fallen into this trap. Getting antsy if I can't fit a run in, worrying that my mood will suddenly crash if I miss a few days. And sometimes you don't even realise it's happening until the enjoyment you take from the run dips a little. I'm a bit obsessive by nature, and when I recognise the need to run take over, I will force myself to take a day off. It doesn't happen often, because I enjoy every run in some way, but I do if sometimes that fades a bit. A coach called Mark Covert ran every day for forty-five years (he ran 163,000 miles) and even HE told his trainees to take a day off once in a while.[14] And nothing bad happens, apart from sometimes feeling a little sluggish. The toolbox has to have other things in it, because life sometimes means we can't get out there every time we want to.

The last pitfall is one that I've never really fallen into, but have thought about on many occasions. And that is becoming a running monk. By that, I mean starting to cut out 'bad' habits to help you progress. Look, I drink wine and eat ice cream and have never worried too much about how much protein I need or how many hours of sleep I'll need for a run. I do all those things because they make me happy and that's important for me after years of dealing with mental-health problems. If you want to get fitter, or feel better, and if cutting out wine and chocolate and late nights does that for you, then GREAT. But if you're removing things from your life in a fairly strict way because you think that running demands it, then stop and think about it. You're not training for a gold medal, you can fit running into your life – don't make your life fit around running. There has to be a balance – we can't all be Gwyneth Paltrow, steaming our vaginas and denying ourselves pizza to make our body a temple. Your mind is the temple. I'm stretching the analogy. So do what feels good, but don't deny yourself anything – you'll still be able to run AND you can have three croissants if that's what you like (and I do).

Be kind to yourself. Make running enjoyable and make it work for YOU – whether that is twice a week for fifteen minutes, or a gradual progression to races and marathons and a level of fitness that will put me to shame. Running works however you need it to work. If you take anything away from this journal, please let it be that.

Write down the things you enjoy doing that seem naughty or unsporty. If they make you happy and don't fuck with your anxiety or mood, then go on and revel in them:

PART TWENTY-ONE

BEING PROUD

OK, write down how your running is going here – and as usual, give yourself one compliment and one target for the next run:

I think I've mentioned just about everything I want to tell you about running and how it can help mental health. The response to *Jog On* really made me want to write down some of the more practical elements of running as a nervous beginner and I *think* I've done that. I hope you're enjoying running, finding it helpful, growing in confidence. I trust you know that you can only run for yourself, and that you should make it enjoyable and not punishing. I hope you've found another tool for the toolbox, one to help your mental health for the rest of your life (or until your knees give out . . . kidding, kidding).

Mental-health issues are painful, isolating and scary. They box us in, make our lives small and take away our hope. I found that running gave me that hope back, opened up the world again and made me feel strong like never before. Oh I hope you've felt a glimmer of that hope. Keep running, keep challenging yourself, keep doing it even when it's hard, or boring, or not as fun as staying in bed. You're giving yourself a new piece of armour against those worries and intrusive thoughts and low moments. It's not a cure-all, it's not a vaccine. It's a tool you work so hard to master, and one which will help you for the rest of your life.

If you've gotten this far, I'm beyond thrilled for you. Write down how you feel – how you could never have imagined you'd have done this before, what you've learnt. And then go for a run (if you want to). Good jogging to you.

Write down absolutely
everything you've
achieved

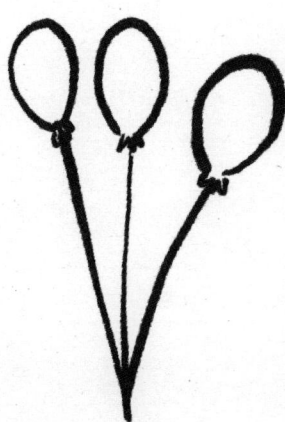

END NOTES

Introduction

1 https://www.runnersworld.com/runners-stories/a20813715/the-obsession-with-running/
2 https://www.pepysdiary.com/indepth/2008/12/12/legends-of-british/
3 https://www.theguardian.com/science/2009/feb/15/psychology-usa
4 http://theconversation.com/to-reduce-stress-and-anxiety-write-your-happy-thoughts-down-99349
5 https://www.pottermore.com/writing-by-jk-rowling/pensieve

Section One

1 https://www.who.int/bulletin/volumes/82/11/en/858.pdf
2 https://www.health.harvard.edu/staying-healthy/understanding-the-stress-response
3 https://www.psychologytoday.com/gb/blog/the-athletes-way/201301/cortisol-why-the-stress-hormone-is-public-enemy-no-1
4 https://psycnet.apa.org/record/2000-08671-001
5 https://www.nature.com/news/2008/080407/full/news.2008.741.html
6 https://www.mentalhealth.org.uk/a-to-z/p/panic-attacks

7 https://anxietynetwork.com/content/what-you-fear-most-cannot-happen

8 https://www.nhs.uk/conditions/panic-disorder/

9 http://www.uhs.nhs.uk/Media/Controlleddocuments/Patient information/Stayinginhospital/Anxietyandbreathing difficulties-patientinformation.pdf

10 https://www.ncbi.nlm.nih.gov/pmc/articles/PMC3181635/

11 http://www.bbc.co.uk/history/british/middle_ages/black disease_01.shtml

12 https://www.kingsfund.org.uk/sites/default/files/field/field_ publication_file/Bringing-together-Kings-Fund-March-2016_1.pdf

13 https://www.washingtonpost.com/news/morning-mix/wp/ 2014/12/12/songs-for-surgeons-a-mixtape-for-the-operating-room/?utm_term=.4dc79a75f04a

14 Suzanne O'Sullivan, *It's All in Your Head*, Chatto & Windus 2015

15 https://www.theguardian.com/society/2015/may/16/you-think-im-mad-the-truth-about-psychosomatic-illness

16 http://www.hse.gov.uk/statistics/causdis/stress.pdf

17 https://www.theguardian.com/lifeandstyle/2019/feb/04/stress-anxiety-knees-weak-palms-sweaty

18 https://www.health.harvard.edu/staying-healthy/anxiety_and_ physical_illness

19 https://www.nhs.uk/conditions/anaphylaxis/

20 https://beta.nhs.uk/find-a-psychological-therapies-service/

21 https://www.nhs.uk/conditions/stress-anxiety-depression/self-help-therapies/

22 https://opinionator.blogs.nytimes.com/2015/05/05/this-is-my-brain-on-pms/

23 http://www.vetstreet.com/our-pet-experts/pets-and-antidepressants-5-reasons-why-your-vet-would-prescribe-them

24 https://www.theguardian.com/society/2019/mar/29/
   antidepressant-prescriptions-in-england-double-in-a-decade
25 https://www.npr.org/sections/health-shots/2014/01/07/26047
   0831/mindfulness-meditation-can-help-relieve-anxiety-and-
   depression?t=1559519767392
26 https://www.anxiety.org/art-helps-treat-anxiety
27 https://www.time-to-change.org.uk/node/100953/
28 https://www.theguardian.com/society/2016/nov/05/men-less-
   likely-to-get-help--mental-health
29 https://news.ok.ubc.ca/2017/11/02/science-confirms-you-
   should-stop-and-smell-the-roses/
30 https://www.theguardian.com/environment/2019/jun/13/two-
   hour-dose-nature-weekly-boosts-health-study-finds
31 https://www.hopkinsmedicine.org/health/wellness-and-
   prevention/exercising-for-better-sleep
32 https://www.theguardian.com/society/2017/sep/06/lack-of-
   sleep-could-contribute-to-mental-health-problems-researchers-
   reveal

Section Two

1 https://www.refinery29.com/en-us/2014/01/60100/women-are-
   intimidated-by-the-gym
2 https://www.runnersworld.com/gear/a20806543/running-shoe-
   questions/
3 https://www.runnersneed.com/expert-advice/gear-guides/
   sports-bra-buying-guide.html
4 http://www2.port.ac.uk/department-of-sport-and-exercise-
   science/research/breast-health/
5 https://www.nhs.uk/live-well/exercise/couch-to-5k-week-by-
   week/
6 https://www.nhs.uk/conditions/chest-pain/

7 https://www.ucl.ac.uk/news/2009/aug/how-long-does-it-take-form-habit

8 Charles Duhigg, *The Power of Habit: Why We Do What We Do*, Random House 2012

9 https://www.nbcnews.com/better/health/why-you-should-work-out-crowd-ncna798936

10 https://www.parkrun.org.uk

11 https://www.thecut.com/2019/01/spending-even-5-minutes-in-nature-can-boost-your-mood.html

12 https://www.ncbi.nlm.nih.gov/pmc/articles/PMC3339578/

13 https://www.scientificamerican.com/article/new-brain-effects-behind-runner-s-high/?redirect=1

14 https://www.covertnevermiss.com/trainers

RESOURCES

Here are some resources that have helped me. If you feel like you need some support, they might help you too.

Websites

https://www.mind.org.uk/ – Providing support for those with mental-health problems, and for their families. Lots of advice, facts and helpful links.

http://www.ocduk.org/ – A website dedicated to help adults and children with OCD. It has great blogs by people who suffer from OCD.

https://www.rcpsych.ac.uk/ – The Royal College of Psychiatry provides information, learning resources and advice on how to navigate issues like work and housing when you have a mental illness.

http://www.ptsduk.org/ – The UK charity which provides support and advice for anyone suffering from PTSD.

https://www.bacp.co.uk/search/Therapists – The British Association for Counselling and Psychotherapy can help you find a qualified therapist.

https://www.runnersworld.co.uk/ – A website stuffed full of amazing stories, tips and routes. Everything you need as a running obsessive.

https://www.nhs.uk/LiveWell/c25k/Pages/couch-to-5k.aspx – The hallowed Couch to 5K programme I've banged on about.

http://www.therunningcharity.org/ – The running charity I was inspired by: go and read about their amazing work.

https://www.thebodypositive.org/ – The site to go to for positive body discussion.

https://youngminds.org.uk/ – A charity specialising in mental-health matters for younger people.

http://www.activityalliance.org.uk/get-active/inclusive-gyms – A site which can point you towards gyms near you which can host those with disabilities.

Apps

Strava – Maps routes and shows you where others go in your area, and lets you keep up with friends who also run.

Couch25K – Coaches you from the first minute of running all the way to 5 kilometres without stopping.

Runkeeper – Saves your running routes and times, and lets you record how you felt during every outing.

MapMyRun – Lets you record your run with a chip in your shoes if you hate taking a phone out when you exercise.

Books

Adam, David, *The Man Who Couldn't Stop* (Picador, 2014).

Askwith, Richard, *Running Free: A Runner's Journey Back to Nature* (Yellow Jersey, 2015).

Austen, Jane, *Pride and Prejudice* (1813; Wordsworth Editions, 1992).

Bretécher, Rose, *Pure* (Penguin, 2015).

Burton, Robert, *The Anatomy of Melancholy* (NYRB Classics, 2001).

Challacombe, Fiona, *Break Free from OCD* (Vermilion, 2011).

Cregan-Reid, Vybarr, *Footnotes: How Running Makes Us Human* (Ebury, 2017).

Emily Dickinson: The Complete Poems (Faber & Faber, 1976).

Fisher, Carrie, *Wishful Drinking* (Simon and Schuster, 2008).

Gordon, Bryony, *Mad Girl* (Headline, 2016).

Harvie, Robin, *Why We Run: A Story of Obsession* (John Murray, 2011).

Heminsley, Alexandra, *Running Like a Girl* (Windmill, 2014).

Kessel, Anna, *Eat, Sweat, Play: How Sport Can Change Our Lives* (Pan Macmillan, 2016).

Mantel, Hilary, *Wolf Hall* (Fourth Estate, 2009).

Menzies-Pike, Catriona, *The Long Run: A Memoir of Loss and Life in Motion* (Penguin Random House 2016).

Morgan, Eleanor, *Anxiety for Beginners* (Pan Macmillan, 2016).

Murakami, Haruki, *What I Talk About When I Talk About Running* (Harvill Secker, 2008).

O'Sullivan, Ronnie, *Running* (Orion, 2013).

Otto, Michael, and Jasper A. J. Smits, *Exercise for Mood and Anxiety: Proven Strategies for Overcoming Depression and Enhancing Well-Being* (Oxford University Press, 2011).

Peterson, Andrea, *On Edge* (Crown Publishing Group, 2017).

Rhodes, James, *Instrumental* (Canongate, 2014).

Rice-Oxley, Mark, *Underneath the Lemon Tree: A Memoir of Depression and Recovery* (Little, Brown, 2012).

Rinpoche, Sakyong Mipham, *Running With The Mind Of Meditation* (Three Rivers Press, 2013).

Stossel, Scott, *My Age of Anxiety: Fear, Hope, Dread, and the Search for Peace of Mind* (Windmill, 2014).

Weekes, Dr Clare, *Self-Help for Your Nerves* (Harper Thorsons, 1995).

Young, Damon, *How to Think About Exercise* (Pan Macmillan, 2014).

ACKNOWLEDGEMENTS

Thank you to everyone at William Collins for helping me make this book. Devising a journal that would be informative and useful without being bossy or saccharine was daunting for me, but the team made it all work.

My lovely editor Tom Killingbeck came up with the idea, and ushered it all through with his usual cheer and patience even when I forgot to answer numerous emails. Olivia Marsden and Helen Upton are a dream to work with on ways to get the book seen by readers, and always have my back. The wonderful illustrations were very loosely based on absurdly bad scribbles I did while writing the book and have been brought to life amazingly by Anna Morrison and I adore them all. Thank you to Rachel Smyth for laying out this journal so beautifully. Thank you to Katy Archer for project editing the journal. I'm very lucky to work with such a lovely group.

Thank you as always to my agent Charlie Campbell for taking me on and helping me to become a writer.

To everyone in my life who helps when I get anxious, sad and wobbly, thanks aren't really enough. But Greg, Lindsay, Alan and Lizzie get them anyway. We all need people who aren't fazed by our mental health low points and I'm hugely lucky with my people.

Lastly, thank you to the stupidest rescue dog in the world. Barney, you made this book almost impossible to write because you never fucking sleep. This has taught me patience and made me learn how to type with one hand while throwing balls with the other.

NOTES

NOTES

NOTES